BRIGITTE BARDOT

Brigitte Bardot

The Legend of
BRIGITTE BARDOT

PETER HAINING

W. H. ALLEN · LONDON
A Howard & Wyndham Company

Printed and bound in Great Britain
by Hazell Watson & Viney Ltd, Aylesbury
for the Publishers, W. H. Allen & Co. Ltd,
44 Hill Street, London W1 X 8LB

ISBN 0 491 03360 5 (W. H. Allen hardcover edition)
ISBN 0 86379 025 9 (Comet Books softcover edition)

'To me, being a blonde meant living my life for
men, being a sex symbol all of the time, a
symbol of carefree, young France. I enjoyed
it, but the blonde hair blinded men to the real
person underneath. I'm taken more seriously
now, and sexually, I please myself more, I ask
much more from men — in part because of my
new identity and because times have changed.
But men still want old-fashioned girlfriends,
so blondes are popular all over again. Before,
I was one of the few top blondes; now there
are so many imitations. It is flattering,
but I've outgrown it.'

Brigitte Bardot

This book is for all the
boys of the class of '56

Contents

Introduction
The Making of a Legend

TODAY, AS ON many other days of the year, Brigitte Bardot will be worshipping the sun and the sea, living casually in their embrace, enjoying the rewards of a remarkable life. For thirty years she herself has been worshipped by an enormous number of fans with the same admiration that was once lavished on the goddesses of Ancient Greece and Rome. For three decades she has been the Aphrodite of the twentieth century.

Few women – or men, for that matter – have led such a public life as 'BB', the initials by which she is widely known, or been the object of such adoration, mixed at times with the most cruel jealousy and malice. For she is not just a beautiful woman, not even just a talented actress: she has become synonymous with a lifestyle that has changed the way many of us think and act. She has been true to herself, to her deepest urges, to her own unique character, and thereby imprinted her image onto the history of this century.

But, this said, do we really *know* Brigitte Bardot? Or is it just a pretty picture we

A favourite photograph – taken in 1957

have in our minds – one that flutters with all the abandoned grace and beauty of a butterfly on the world's cinema screens? Can the woman herself be like the goddess we see projected before us – for Screen Goddess she certainly was, and still remains, thirty years from the day when she made her film début and, incredible as it may seem, almost on the eve of her fiftieth birthday. Other sex symbols have come and gone – Jane Russell, Anita Ekberg, Jayne Mansfield – but BB lives on, her fame enduring and her legend secure. And even at a time when she might be expected to have retired from public view – though she has more than once attempted to do just that – she continues to contemplate projects for the future, involves herself in national wildlife campaigns, and attracts the attention of the media with the same consuming interest as always. Still, too, she draws the photographers' lenses – those same lenses that have revealed her over the years to be arguably the most photogenic, and photographed, woman of the twentieth century. No other woman of our times, with the possible exception of Marilyn Monroe, has so loved the camera and been so loved by it in return.

Even the most casual visitor to St. Tropez in the south of France will have no difficulty in appreciating why BB the sun-worshipper should have chosen to live here

– and by so doing transform the life and character of this former Provençal fishing village on the beautiful Var coast. The sun burns down on a curve of dazzling white sand lapped by the deep azure blue of the Mediterranean. The hot climate is, though tempered by the winds off the sea, and occasionally the calm is disturbed by the blast of the *mistral*.

Before St. Tropez became a haunt of the rich and famous, before the hundreds of thousands of tourists began flooding in each year, its tall, old houses with their multi-coloured walls stood huddled in the *Pesquiere*, the original fishermen's port, with the nearby remnants of the old fortifications. Both are reminders that though St. Tropez may be generally thought of as one of the most fashionable places in Europe – the 'Mecca of the Bikini' as one writer dubbed it – it actually has a long and intriguing history.

A community has actually existed on the south shore at the tip of the bay known as the St. Tropez Gulf since the days of the Greeks who called it Attenopolis. It was re-named St. Tropez about the year 305 and after a period in the hands of Saracen invaders, developed into a prosperous trading port. Although its position always made it vulnerable to attack from Africa, the fortifications which its inhabitants built proved impregnable to most assaults, and it was not until World War II when the joint Franco-American landings took place, that it suffered serious damage. In the years which followed, St. Tropez was rebuilt, and began to attract favourable attention from visiting writers and painters. As if heralding the arrival of Brigitte Bardot herself, that grand lady of French letters, Colette, while living in the town, wrote in her *La Naissance du Jour* that here, 'a woman may claim as many native countries as she has had happy love affairs; she is also reborn beneath each sky where she recovers from the pain of loving.' And as you will discover through the pages of this book, it would be hard to find a description which more neatly matches what BB has sought from her adopted home.

The house where Brigitte lives, a villa named *La Madrague*, is located just outside the town right on the beach of the Bay des Caroubiers, and surrounded by high walls of concrete and bamboo fencing which run right down to the water's edge. The grounds are entered through a large, wrought-iron gate, and the house itself is half-hidden by trees and tall beach grass. It is a handsome, though not ostentatious, ochre-coloured building with floor-to-ceiling windows and a huge patio. There is also a compound for Brigette's pets as well as a good-sized swimming pool.

Inside, *La Madrague* is simply but comfortably furnished with modern fixtures and fittings: souvenirs from Brigitte's trips abroad decorate the rooms, and a number of striking paintings adorn the walls – some she has painted herself and which display an eye for line and colour. The lady of the house's various pets have the run of the place, and the dogs in particular tend to follow their mistress as she moves about from room to room. Brigitte enjoys a quiet and unhurried daily routine, and house guests are generally expected to fit in with this casual way of life. When it comes to meals, Brigitte prefers simple dishes, with a crisp

Brigitte at 21 – what does the future hold?

salad and chilled white wine among her favourites.

Out in the spacious, sandy grounds, Brigitte likes to sunbathe for hours on end – occasionally nude – afterwards plunging into the ocean for a brisk, refreshing swim. Because of the hordes of tourists that come hoping for a glimpse of her, she also owns a small boat which she uses to slip away unnoticed to bathe in some secluded cove when the intruders become too persistent. (For example, one American tourist firm for a while advertised its holidays in St. Tropez with a promise of a boat trip past BB's home 'where she frequently bathes *au naturale!*')

Brigitte's decision to settle in St. Tropez came as a direct result of the film which made her world-famous, *And God Created Woman*, shot in 1956. Much of it was filmed during the summer on what was then a deserted beach of the small, unspoiled village – and during her stay she fell in love with the place. When she bought *La Madrague* shortly afterwards, it changed the character of the whole area, as travel writer Patrick Turnbull wrote in 1972: 'The meteoric rise in popularity of the Var coast during the last two decades is principally due to that of St. Tropez, which in turn owes much of its success to a young film actress, the blonde Brigitte Bardot, often described in the early fifties as the "Sex Kitten" and one of the first to display her totally uncovered natural charms on the screen. Her villa, *La Madrague*, became the centre of the younger set at the time, this automatically drawing the crowds not only from France, but from all over Western Europe and even from the United States, hoping to see and copy their idol, feeling too that by breaking new ground and condemning resorts that were fashionable prewar they were hammering further nails into

Even behind the walls of her St. Tropez home, the photographers still clamour after her

14

the coffin-lid of *la monde de papa.*'

But if St. Tropez is famous because of BB, what is it that has made BB herself so famous? The answer is not just her films, for among the acclaimed and notorious ones there have also been some undoubtedly poor ones. Nor is it just the incredible and widespread international publicity that has focused on her every activity – as movie star, as sex symbol, and lover. No – the simple answer to the question is Brigitte *herself*. This uniquely beautiful lady whose face and figure are among the most instantly recognisable of the age and would have made her unforgettable whatever she chose to be.

Those who have known her during the past three eventful decades say that little about her has changed. She still has that mixture of innocence and bold sexuality in her face. Watching her move gives you an uncanny feeling that the God who created her made her epitomise everything that men of any age admire and appreciate in female anatomy.

It would be a mistake, though, to think that Brigitte was not fully aware of her impact on people, or that she did not know exactly how to make the very best of herself. For as she says, 'Sex appeal cannot be measured. It's the way the mind controls the body.'

But despite an image based on petulant sensuality, Brigitte Bardot is no dumb blonde. Her mind is quick and perceptive; her IQ is high and her wit can be devastating. To have survived almost fifty years of the extraordinary life that fate has dealt her without a natural intelligence would have been quite impossible.

In appearance, Brigitte is tall (5ft 7ins) and willowy, she still has an excellent figure, slim waist, full breasts, and a golden coloured skin from her dedicated sun-worship. To keep this way, she says, she does not have to diet, perform special exercises, or even use creams. She is indeed fortunate!

The famous face now contains a few lines, of course, and the green–flecked brown eyes are very knowing, very penetrating when she stares. The once tangled, corn-coloured hair which became her trademark has been allowed to return to its natural colour – in between very light-brown and dark blonde. The little nose is dabbed with a few attractive freckles, and as always the only make-up she uses is for her eyes. Her lips still have that luscious pout which makes everyone who meets her feel she is just about to kiss them. (She is, in fact, credited with having started the fad among film and theatrical people of greeting each other with a kiss even if they have never met before.) Nowadays, though, BB touches the tips of one of her fingers to her lips and brushes this against the cheek of a friend. To others she merely offers her small, delicate right hand with the ease and grace of a monarch offering it to a courtier. But she does so with politeness, rather than any sense of superiority. When she speaks, her voice is low and musical, though when addressing English and American journalists it can break into a superb fractured English that makes her allure even more devastating.

Brigitte has never been one to follow fashions, although she does like her clothes to be smart and well made. She prefers pastel colours and generally loose-fitting garments. She also likes jeans and boots, and although she possesses a large collection of shoes and sandals, often goes barefoot at home. Best of all, she likes the freedom of nudity.

'I prefer to be naked in the sun,' she says. 'When I have to dress, I dress informally. I don't care what the fashions are. I dress in what I know suits me, even if it is called out of fashion.' Fate, of course, played a trick on her when her studious avoidance of any of the current fashions in the late fifties and sixties made her one of the most copied women of the day. As Gerard Fairlie wrote in October 1960: 'She clearly has a far greater influence, in her own right, than the great fashion houses, because she is prepared to defy their more ludicrous creations, or indeed any trends they may stress, if she thinks that they won't suit her. And as a result she is copied by infinitely more women than buy the extravagant originals created by the fashion houses.' (Although her style of dress is no longer in such vogue, the skilfully coiffered untidy hairstyle which she originated is still much in evidence today.)

But Brigitte is very interested in what goes on in the world. She reads books, newspapers and magazines voraciously, though she rarely watches television or goes to the cinema. Like many women, she loves window shopping. 'It is one of the pleasures of life, isn't it?' she says. 'But it is very difficult for me. If I go to a shop, five minutes later there are twenty people trying to look at me. The result is that I look at magazines at home and send my secretary to buy the things I like.

'You know what I'd love to do? Perhaps it's silly, but I'd like to go to the Galeries Lafayette incognito and just walk about. Or else sit peacefully on the terrace of a café . . . But it isn't possible. And when people gather round I no longer feel free. I stop being myself. What can I do? Only stay home in my "bubble" as one of my friends calls it.'

The matter of friendship has always been a difficult one for Brigitte. 'How can a person like me have many friends?' she says. 'Real friends? Acquaintances of course by the thousand. But sincere friendship comes only slowly. And I have to separate those who like me for myself from those who want something from Brigitte Bardot.'

One of her most enduring friendships has been with Roger Vadim, her first husband, and the director who made the film, *And God Created Woman*, which made them both famous. Their lives are very much entwined, although their paths often diverge. Somehow destiny always seems to bring them back together again for one reason or another.

Speaking about Brigitte not so long ago, Vadim said: 'She has the courage to be what she is. She goes to the limit in everything without calculating what will happen there. When she leaves one lover for another, nothing remotely hypocritical stops her. She has a bit of the Don Juan in her. When she tells a boy she loves him she is entirely sincere – but she can forget him the next day . . . She is truly modest. I've seen her sobbing before a mirror, insisting she wasn't at all pretty! She has simple tastes: a private house, the sun, a garden, a few pets – that's enough to make her happy.'

Because of her fame, Brigitte is only too well aware of the problems inherent in meeting someone new, as she told another of her friends, the writer Françoise Sagan. 'The man who's going to meet me says to himself, "I am going to meet Brigitte Bardot," and he starts worrying, he's petrified. And I say to myself, "He's coming to meet Brigitte Bardot, this woman I don't know!" and I stop being natural. Or else there are the journalists. If I go out with a

16

guy they don't know, they'll follow me for hours and the next day they will write "BB's new fiancé" or "BB's new lover". It's awful.' (One effect of fame is that Brigitte Bardot sees herself as two quite distinct personalities.)

Love has always been of paramount importance to Brigitte – indeed it is at the very core of her nature. As she explains, 'For me love needs mystery, secrecy, silence. It is a private, very rich and complex affair that's very simple at the same time. The more I hear about all those perversions and accessories, the less I want to make love. I think that exhibitionism is repressed shame . . .

'Basically I'm really a dreadfully normal person. I know I'm healthy. I don't take drugs – I'm even terribly afraid of them. Why destroy oneself slowly? One might as well kill oneself right out. Drugs are a slow death, total slavery – and I detest being a slave. I like making love with the man I love, just the two of us and no one else, so I must be really "square" right? When love dies,' says Brigitte, 'I never see old lovers. My friends are my friends. My love is my love. It is a pity to be friends with a lover. It's giving him a second part of yourself. I'm not interested in that kind of friendship. When my passion dies I just go.'

Brigitte has always hated to be – as she describes it – contrainte, obligated to anyone. No one knows this better than her redoubtable and at the same time motherly Paris agent, Olga Horstig-Primus who explains, 'She regards a dinner date arranged a week in advance as a prison sentence. She will only live for the moment.' Brigitte readily agrees: 'I never organise my future, for it is the surest way to forget living in the present.'

Madame Horstig-Primus has long been aware that her client considers acting as of secondary importance in her life, and has more than once expressed the view that for years her job merely consisted of saying 'No!' to all projects that were offered to Brigitte. BB explains her philosophy towards acting in this manner: 'First,' she says, 'I am a woman, and only second an actress. I am not like some actresses who only come alive when they are in front of the movie camera. I live when I am *not* filming. I am a better actress if the director takes hold of me and is masterful. I like that. Some people think you have to be old and ugly before they will say you are good. I prefer to be beautiful and not so good.'

While at her busiest as an actress, Brigitte admitted that filming was always an agony to her. 'You know, I don't really have acting in my blood. I'd say to myself, "In two months, we start; in one month; in one week." Then, bang! I'd get spots. So we'd have to wait a bit and I'd say to myself, "I've gained that much time!" During each film I was frantic – and yet I have done more than forty. One would have thought I was a beginner who had never set foot on a set. I think it's shyness that makes me like that. And then I don't know how to apply myself, to prepare my parts. It comes by itself or it doesn't come at all. I'm not a real actress, I think, or a good audience either. Not at least for the movies.'

Extraordinary words, perhaps, for a woman who has become a cinema legend in her own lifetime. A screen goddess recognised by audiences all over the world. But then Brigitte Bardot is no ordinary person – she is an enigma as well as a phenomenon. She personifies fame in capital letters. Way beyond mere international acclaim, with screaming crowds at airports, police protection for every move, open doors to the world's leaders – *there* lies a unique kind of celebrity. For a man or woman is truly famous when they become a universal yardstick for excellence in their own field, a handy metaphor more than a human being.

Where money is mentioned, for example, Paul Getty stands for unimaginable riches; while Picasso serves for artistic genius. And what car driver has not yelled at another who cuts in front of him in traffic, 'Who the hell do you think you are – Stirling Moss?' And in all three cases this occurs despite the fact that other generations of money makers, painters and racing drivers have succeeded those three.

By these standards, then, is Brigitte Bardot not one of the most famous women of the century? Her initials have indeed become synonymous with a whole range of attitudes. And her provocative figure, her hairstyle, her pout, all have combined to give harassed mothers the world over a phrase with which to reprimand their daughters: 'Who do you think you are — Brigitte Bardot?'

Encapsulated in that phrase are many facets of her incredible life – the broken marriages, the highly publicised love affairs, the whole range of sensational newspaper stories – but all without the remorse and retribution that such acts usually bring. Though much that she has done has caused shudders among those who like to uphold the conventions of society, her emotional upheavals have also had a tremendous *chic* about them, becoming a kind of blueprint for the 'beautiful people'. Indeed, the very consistency of her behaviour over the years has given a certain respectability to such activities.

Unquestionably, though, Brigitte's greatest achievement has been to sustain her legend over thirty years to the very threshold of her half century. Many other celebrities have burst upon the scene during this same time span, burned brightly, then disappeared into oblivion, or become just a footnote in contemporary history. In the female stakes, only Marilyn Monroe can be compared to Brigitte Bardot. But then Monroe died young and tragically. And remember, too, that Brigitte packed most of her filmic achievements into one tumultuous period, yet despite her comparative inactivity since, her reputation continues to grow.

Back in 1960, when her legend had not long been assured, Brigitte was asked when she would write her autobiography. Those who know her have spoken of her command of language and ability to write flowing, literate prose. Her third husband, the German playboy, Gunther Sachs, for instance, said, 'She is a woman of high intelligence, a superb writer who conveys the intensity of her feelings in beautiful, erotic letters.' So what could be more natural than for her to put the record straight about the millions of headlines she has generated? But BB was not interested. 'How can I write my memoirs yet,' she said. 'Perhaps when I am fifty . . .'

Now, as she nears that age, there are signs that she might do just that – but in the interim I should like to offer my own study of the life and legend of Brigitte Bardot. It is told to quite a large extent through her own words, given year by year as the events and emotions she describes were taking place. It catches her changing moods and opinions throughout the tragedies and the

Brigitte, the stunning young starlet

BRIGITTE BARDOT

excitements of these years. It is also based on the comments and observations of those closest to her – in particular her mother, her three husbands, and various men and women from the world of films as well as certain trusted journalists. Their intimate observations of BB the public celebrity and Brigitte Bardot the private person give us a rather clearer picture of the woman and her motivations. Certainly the range of the book, almost five decades in her life, is more wide-ranging than any work previously attempted.

From all these words emerges a woman who can be highly unpredictable, spoiled, demanding and petulant – but at the same time affectionate, loyal, brave, determined, likable and highly lovable. A woman who has truly earned the legendary status which now surrounds her. As she herself said recently, 'A person like myself cannot buy experience cheaply. I wouldn't have changed a thing in my life, including all the heartache and the catastrophes. I believe I am a better person. And when I am old it is my character that I will have to live by.'

Here, then, is a record in words and pictures of just *how* that experience was bought and that character formed.

Bordeira, Portugal
September 1982

Still a headline-maker in 1982 as she campaigns for animals

1934-1951
A Girl Called 'Bri-Bri'

Passy, THE EIGHTH arrondisse-ment of Paris, has changed lit-tle over the past half century. It is a prosperous and fashionable district, a stronghold of the French upper-middle-class. These people, with their strict conventions, elegant life-style, and refined speech, are part of the backbone of Parisian culture.

At the heart of this district lies the Ave-nue de la Bourdonnais, bounded by the famous landmarks of the Champ de Mars, the Eiffel Tower and the River Seine. The Avenue reflects the sophisticated world of its inhabitants – men in the senior echelons of banking, of commerce and the arts. And it was in one of the tall, grey apartment houses on the left-hand side of the street, number 35, in a luxurious apartment on the fifth floor, that Brigitte Bardot was born around midday on 28 September 1934, a bright warm autumn morning. The blonde-haired child with big, sleepy eyes, weighed seven pounds six ounces, and was named after her mother's favourite child-hood doll.

Brigitte's parents were, on the surface,

archetypal examples of the residents of Passy. Her father, Louis Bardot, was a prosperous industrialist, with a liquid gas factory at Aubervillers. A bespectacled, slightly austere man devoted to routine and good manners, Louis Bardot greeted the arrival of his first child with delight – mixed with a little apprehension at the feelings of unrest building up all over Europe, particu-larly in Germany. His wife, Anne-Marie, whose maiden name was Muscel, was something of a contrast. She displayed similar reserve and culture but nursed a strong interest in music and dance, having studied acting and dancing in Milan during her youth. Her attempts at a theatrical career had, however, been frustrated and there was always a feeling of suppressed emotions when the subject emerged. These feelings were later to play a crucial part in the development of Mme Bardot's baby daughter.

The Bardots proved a tightly-knit family during the early years of Brigitte's child-hood, and in 1939 another daughter, Marie-Jeanne, was born. In the manner of families all over the world, the Bardots delighted in pet names for each other – father and mother became Pilou and Totty, Brigitte was Bri-Bri and the younger child, Mijanou.

Like most other children from her back-ground, Brigitte's early years were spent in

Scarcely in her teens, 'Bri-Bri' is already a beauty

the charge of a governess: first an English nurse and later a Frenchwoman. It was the departure of the English nurse that first made her aware of a change in her world. War had broken out across Europe and soon most of France, including Paris, was in German hands. Today, she still recalls the period vividly.

'The war *was* my childhood,' Brigitte says. 'It comes back to me when I feel worried or in a bad mood. I remember the alerts in Paris, being awakened in the middle of the night. And then I was especially afraid of the basement we had to go to – I felt trapped. I was afraid of dying there. I'm still terribly claustrophobic.'

During the period of the Occupation there were, however, bright, sunlit days she remembered. Walking beneath the shady trees of the Champ de Mars . . . sitting beside the sparkling Seine . . . pushing her baby sister's pram along the Bois de Boulogne. She did not go short of anything, either, for Papa Bardot's business continued to flourish despite the oppressive presence of the German forces. She was spoiled with a host of dolls and toys, and pet animals which were to become an enduring love.

As their two daughters began to grow, Bardot *mère et père* moved across the Seine from the Avenue de la Bourdonnais to an even larger and more sumptuous nine-room apartment at number 1 Rue de la Pompe, a stone's throw from the Bois de Boulogne. The family was increased by the presence of two servants, but daily life continued in a well-ordered and rigidly supervised pattern for Brigitte and Marie-Jeanne.

Brigitte's education began at home with her French governess, but at seven years of age she was sent to Hattemar, an expensive private school in the sixteenth arrondissement. However, Mme Bardot still dreamed of her own artistic past, and if she could no longer dance or act herself, at least she would give her daughter the chance to. At first, Brigitte was given dancing instruction at home by Recco, a member of the Opera Ballet. But when she needed more space to develop she was enrolled at a small dance studio run by a Madame Bourget in the Rue Spotini.

Brigitte, away from the confines of her day-to-day existence, took to dancing with unbounded delight and quickly proved herself an adept pupil, ever anxious to learn. However, although the dancing lessons gave Brigitte a sense of freedom and a chance to express herself, she continued to be a very reserved child, shy and self-conscious. She had few friends and was rarely allowed to visit other girls' homes. This is how she recalls that period of her life:

'I was timid and self-effacing. To make matters worse I was ugly. My hair was thin. I wore spectacles. I had to have a brace on my teeth. And I even got eczema whenever I was especially worried. I was always paralysed with fear when my parents invited their friends' children round for parties or took me out on their social calls. In Paris, in that class, many parents were strict, but mine were stricter than most. They wanted me to become a very well-educated, cultured and, I think, rather boring girl. My education was both severe and indulgent. It left me quite unprepared for life as I found it. I hated lessons, but I worked hard because my parents wished me to do well.'

In the light of these comments, it is perhaps not surprising that she threw herself into her dancing with such determination – or that she got such pleasure from her success. It is also interesting to reflect what a contrast her background was to that of the other great sex symbol of our times, Marilyn Monroe. As journalist Frank Law has written, 'It was so different from that of Marilyn who hardly knew her own mother, whose early years were passed facing the hard reality of the orphanage, and a succession of foster-parents.' Law goes on, 'For both girls, however, a career in films was a chance to revolt. In Marilyn's case, against poverty and a feeling of being unwanted. In Brigitte's, against a stifling, upper-crust code of behaviour with which she was out of sympathy.'

In 1947, aged thirteen, Brigitte took the entrance exam to the highly prestigious National Conservatory of Music and Dancing. She was one of 150 eager teenagers who sought desperately to impress – and she was one of only eight who were accepted. It was like a dream come true! There and then Brigitte determined she would become a great ballerina, and quickly set about impressing her teacher, a Russian exile named Boris Kniazeff. Under his guidance she began to develop a style and grace that would ultimately enable her to make a living as a ballerina had she chosen such a career. Indeed, it was from Kniazeff that Brigitte learned her graceful and sensual walk which was later to have such a shattering impact when she arrived on the cinema screen.

But despite her rapidly developing talent as a dancer, fate had destined that Brigitte Bardot was to succeed in a quite different field. However, she came upon her destiny in a roundabout way. A year later, in 1948, Madame Bardot, who had grown tired of inactivity now that both her daughters were growing up, decided to open a bouti-que in the Rue de la Pompe. After all the restrictions of the war years, France – and Paris in particular – was ready for a new upsurge in fashion, and Anne-Marie's decision quickly proved a most opportune one.

The years of dedication to dancing had also worked a transformation on Brigitte. Gone was the bespectacled, buck-toothed, pig-tailed little girl: she was now a slim and lithe young woman who carried herself well, 'piquant and sexy' to quote one biographer. She also looked good in the latest junior fashions. Not slow to sense an opportunity, Mme Bardot began to dress her daughter in clothes that were sold in her boutique, and Brigitte, for her part, knew instinctively how to show them and herself to the best advantage. The result was a steady stream of customers beating a path to the little shop on the Rue de la Pompe – as well as the first of a growing circle of admiring young men.

After a while, Mme Bardot became aware that the garments of one particular supplier, a young *modiste* called Jean Barthet, not only looked particularly good on her daughter but were selling well to her customers. When, early in 1949, she learned that Barthet was planning a fashion show at the Drouand David Gallery in the heart of the Faubourg St. Honoré, she suggested to him that a novel way of presenting his new line would be to link each design to a dance step. And who could better model such clothes than her ballerina daughter, Brigitte?

Barthet jumped at the idea, and on 29 January 1949, Brigitte Bardot made her first public appearance as a fashion model in the glittering surroundings of the famous Parisian picture gallery. The fifteen-year-old girl was an immediate success – her pretty gamine features and lithe movements entrancing the buyers and the photographers and journalists from fashion magazines who were present. One in particular took a careful note of her performance, as Mme Bardot herself was to recall when talking of her daughter's break into the world of modelling.

There was no immediate response to her appearance, however, and it was not until two months later, on a blustery March day that a phone call to the Bardot household – telephone number JASmin 82-86 – set in motion the crucial events which were to put the teenage girl on the first steps to stardom. Brigitte was just coming in the front door after her lessons at Hattemar when the phone rang. Her mother picked up the receiver to find that her husband's cousin, a Mme de la Villuchet was on the line. Mme Bardot was fond of the younger woman, and both shared a keen interest in fashion. Mme de la Villuchet worked on the popular French magazine *Jardin des Modes*, and was editor of the 'Junior Miss' section.

After the usual pleasantries, the caller said to Mme Bardot: 'I'm in a real fix. I do hope you can help me out. The young girl who was to pose for me this afternoon has got scarlet fever. May I borrow Brigitte? She is pretty and just the type I want for the picture.' Brigitte, who had been standing in the hallway listening to the conversation, immediately began to nod her head in agreement. Could she do it, please? she silently implored her mother. For a moment Mme Bardot hesitated, and then relented. After all what harm could come from just one fashion photograph? She told Mme de la Villuchet that they would be right along to the offices of the magazine.

'It was all over in five minutes,' Mme Bardot said afterwards, 'I didn't think anything of it at the time. Then a few weeks later I got another phone call from a woman's magazine.' The voice on the end of the line this time was demanding, but still tactful. It also carried the kind of authority that working for *the* most prestigious woman's magazine in France gave to its employees. The voice was that of Madame Lazareff, the editor of *Elle*.

Madame Lazareff explained that she had seen Brigitte's picture in *Jardin des Modes*. 'We know your daughter is not a professional model,' she said, 'and doesn't pose for cover pictures. But just this once would you allow her to? She's exactly the type of young teenager we need for next week's cover. But don't worry, there won't be any publicity, we'll just use her initials, Mlle BB.'

Remembering this conversation, Mme Bardot says 'I let myself be persuaded. Perhaps I did the wrong thing. But Brigitte was jumping up and down with excitement. The whole thing was a great game to her. Brigitte was never a professional cover girl. Like any girl of fifteen she was thrilled to see her picture on the front cover of a magazine. She used to walk by the kiosk at the corner of the street, dragging her school friends with her. "Look," I can remember her saying, "see that, it's me. That's me on the cover."'

The front cover photograph of Brigitte appeared on the issue of 2 May 1949. Although she was only wearing a simple plaid dress, there was no concealing her rapidly maturing woman's body: the narrow waist, the full breasts thrust provocatively forward and complemented by a

Modelling gave Brigitte her first step into the public eye

sulky and rather suggestive pout of the lips – actually brought on by nervousness! However, though the picture may well have impressed her friends, the reaction at home was rather different. On first sight of the cover, Mme Bardot admitted she had immediate reservations about what she had done – but Bardot *père* was furious! Modelling for magazine photographs was not his idea of what the well-brought up daughter of an influential businessman should be seen doing! Brigitte posing was to be an emotive subject in the apartment in Rue de la Pompe in the months which followed.

A day or two after *Elle*, complete with Brigitte on the cover, hit the news-stands of France, an express letter arrived at the Bardot home. It was addressed to Brigitte, and her mother recalls that it said something like, 'Would you like to go into films? If you would, and it would interest you to make a test, telephone me. My name is Marc Allegret.'

Allegret was something of a legend in French film circles. He was the creator of the famous film, *Lac aux Dames*, made in 1934, which had given the screen one of its first sex symbols, Simone Simon. Could it be that he had seen something as unique in the young cover girl as he had when he first spotted Simone Simon?

Madame Bardot initially wanted to reject the approach out of hand, but once again the pleading of her young daughter made her reluctantly agree to go and see Allegret at his apartment house just off the Champs-Elysées. She recalls: 'I decided to play the heavy mother because I didn't really want her to go into films at all. I wanted her to keep on dancing. And it went off just like that.'

Madame Bardot remained implacable as Allegret tried to get her to agree to a film test for her daughter. While the couple talked, Brigitte sat nervously on the edge of her chair, unable to keep her eyes off the young man sitting beside the film maker. He was thin, casually dressed, had long, dark hair and a rather soulful face.

It was not until later that Brigitte was to learn who this young man was. His name was Roger Vladimir Plemiannikov, and he was a twenty-two-year-old penniless Russian émigré who had come to France in the hope of making a career as a screen-writer and, ultimately, a film director. He had done a little acting and then attached himself to Allegret in the hope of fulfilling his dreams. Instead, it was to be the fifteen-year-old girl who faced him nervously across Allegret's well-furnished apartment who was to help him accomplish his desire. The young man was destined to become famous as Roger Vadim.

Although Marc Allegret did his best to make Mme Bardot change her mind, she proved equally stubborn in her refusal to be budged. Finally, he stood up and said, 'Well, madame, suppose we leave things as they are?' Although Brigitte was naturally disappointed at her mother's decision, she couldn't keep thoughts of the dark-haired young man out of her mind. As they walked home, she said, 'Mother, did you notice that queer-looking man? He's got a very odd face, don't you think?' 'That's true,' Madame Bardot had replied, 'He is a curious-looking young man.'

Brigitte's mother continues the next part of the story. 'As far as I was concerned the incident was over and finished with. That was in July. In September my husband and I went on holiday to Biarritz, leaving Brigitte, my younger daughter, Mijanou, and my mother in our apartment. We had been away about a week when I got a telephone call from my mother, who said, "There are some funny things going on. There's a most extraordinary young man, very strange indeed, who keeps on coming to the apartment. He spends hours with Brigitte. He says he is rehearsing her for a film test she is to make for Marc Allegret." Oh, indeed, I thought, and decided I'd better come back to Paris at once to see what was going on. I found Vadim, who by then had got quite a hold on my daughter – and she was fascinated by him'.

Brigitte herself has also confessed her feelings when meeting Vadim: 'I could not take my eyes off him. He seemed so strange. He talked as if the world were his, and everything he said was fascinating. We flirted. It wasn't the first time I had flirted, even though I was only fifteen. But up to that time my flirtations had not been serious.'

Begrudgingly, Mme Bardot now agreed to the film test taking place – secretly convincing herself that nothing would come of it. Amazingly – in the light of Brigitte's subsequent career – *Mamam* was right! Allegret chose for the test a scene from a film script called *Les Lauriers Sont Coupes*, which his young assistant Roger Vladimir Plemiannikov had written. He also had the young émigré play opposite her. Despite the fact that Brigitte had already revealed herself as being photogenic and a lithe and sinuous dancer, her performance before the movie camera was wooden and uninspiring. Marc Allegret shook his head sadly. The girl whose face had so attracted him on the magazine cover just couldn't act, he told himself.

And so Brigitte returned to her school and her dancing, and Vadim to his Bohemian existence. But *something* had now convinced the Russian that she could be a

star if handled properly.

Madame Bardot once more returns to the story of those crucial months in the autumn of 1949 and on into 1950. 'A lot of nonsense has been written about Vadim acting as a kind of Svengali to Brigitte, moulding her into a completely different being. That's not true at all. At the time he met Brigitte he was anxious to launch his career, as all young people are. He saw in Brigitte a means of doing so. They were in love, and for him it was both a personal and a professional relationship. Like a tandem bicycle, you know. He made her give up her dancing lessons and leave school before she got her *Bachot*. I wanted her to go on with her dancing and get her *Bachot* – after all, a diploma is always a diploma. But Brigitte was in love and wanted to do everything he wanted.'

Brigitte had already secretly decided that her developing figure would disqualify her from being either a ballet dancer or a model. She says that on her fifteenth birthday she stood naked in front of her mirror and examined every inch of her body. 'A tiny waist – yes, that would be all right,' she recalls telling herself. 'Legs – yes, they were all right as well. But my bosom! They'd never accept a bosom like mine. I had twice too much. And with my nineteen-inch waist, it looked ridiculous!'

The love affair between the two young people soon ran into stormy waters. Brigitte's father warned her off Vadim with a mixture of accusations and threats – all to no avail. Even a period of separation when Marc Allegret took his young friend to London to assist him in filming a picture called *Blanche Fury* did nothing to dampen her desire. She pleaded with her parents to allow them to be married, or at least get engaged. But, still only sixteen years old, she was told firmly that any such thing was quite out of the question until she was at least eighteen. Then, when Vadim decided to go to the South of France for a while to finish a film script he was working on, it seemed like the end of the world to the unhappy young woman. And so, one evening while the Bardots were out on a drive, Brigitte, alone and desperate, attempted to commit suicide by putting her head in the gas oven.

Fortunately, Mme Bardot had what she later described as a 'maternal presentiment' about her daughter's state of mind, and she and her husband cut short their drive to return home. They reached the apartment and found the unconscious girl just in time.

As it later transpired, this was not to be the last time Brigitte would try to take her own life . .

The attempted suicide undoubtedly changed the Bardots' attitude to Vadim, even if only out of a desire to try and save their daughter from any more such dramas, and on his almost immediate return to Paris after hearing the news, he was granted unhindered access to Brigitte and her home. Now he could concentrate his efforts on getting her the acting career which, he believed, would ultimately help him fulfil his own ambitions. Apart from his own coaching, he had Brigitte take lessons at a drama school run by René Simon. He also encouraged her to take other modelling and photographic assignments and looked for opportunities among his contacts in the

The Bardot family at home: father, Louis (left), grandfather, and mother, Anne-Marie, with the young Roger Plémiannikov, who was to change their daughter's life so dramatically

30

French film business to get her another chance before the cameras.

Then in the spring of 1952, with Brigitte still six months away from her eighteenth birthday, Vadim landed her her first small part in a film to be made by the busy and popular director, Jean Boyer. Fearing another disaster if she was asked to make a film test, Vadim coerced Boyer into watching his protégée at work at René Simon's studio. Although Boyer also, apparently, asked to see the Allegret test, he confessed that he found himself sharing some of Vadim's enthusiasm for Brigitte's rapidly flowering, sensual beauty as soon as he saw her. 'A lot could be done with that girl' he said simply.

The first chapter in the thirty remarkable years of the superstar we know as BB was just about to begin . . .

The budding ballet dancer – Brigitte with her teacher, Boris Kniazeff

1952
'Crazy for Love'

As Mme Bardot had already quite correctly suspected, Roger Vadim saw more in Brigitte than a girl with whom he would just fall in love. As she later confessed, 'My daughter, with her typical religious and bourgeois upbringing, excited Vadim. He once said to me, "That's the amusing thing, to take a girl like her and make it appear as if she has gone completely off the rails."'

From the moment Vadim had first caught sight of Brigitte in Marc Allegret's flat, she had impressed herself forcefully onto his consciousness. And very soon he was beginning to realise she might be the means of fulfilling his dream. He recalls their meeting vividly: 'Two things struck me about her, then. First, her style. She had a way to be very free with her body. And her mind. When I say free with her body, I'm talking about the way she would walk, move, look at people, sit. She was a fantastic classical dancer – and she had the sort of grace and elegant movement that good, classic dancers have. She was also, for a little bourgeoise, in a certain way very revolutionary. She approached life, any kind of

The bikini which caused Brigitte's father to go to court when he saw her in *The Lighthouse Keeper's Daughter*

problem, with a really free mind.'

There was also something eerily prophetic about their meeting, Vadim says. 'She was the living image of the heroine of my first novel, written when I was a boy. I called it *The Wise Sophie*, and the way she spoke – almost, it seemed, in whole phrases from the book.' (Later Brigitte was to refer to herself – and sign her love letters to Roger Vadim – with the words 'Your little Sophie'.)

When, by the spring of 1952, Vadim was being reluctantly accepted in the Bardot household, he cemented this acceptance by getting himself a regular job on the popular magazine, *Paris Match*. 'I had to convince Brigitte's parents that I had some kind of regular income,' he said. 'When I first met her I was an unknown assistant to a film producer and not doing very well. For three years before that I was an actor. Not a very good one, but it gave me experience that was valuable.'

Although Vadim's position on *Paris Match* was as a writer-photographer, colleagues at the time remember him as a rather fervent young man talking endlessly to anyone who would listen about his idea of the 'new woman' – and waxing lyrical over the young girl he had found to make this ideal become flesh, the seventeen-year-old Brigitte Bardot.

Despite his gushing enthusiasm, Vadim

had his thoughts very clearly marshalled. 'I had an idea of the type of woman I was looking for,' he said. 'I wanted to express a certain type of femininity which I thought was new. Women have always been conditioned to a form of slavery towards men. Ultimately the man may become the slave, but it doesn't begin that way. In the past women have achieved their power over men in a variety of purely feminine ways – using charm, coquetry, trickery if you like. But I feel that the young girl of today – the sixteen- and seventeen-year-old – has a masculine mind. She wants to be free to love as a man does. I am not speaking of the career woman, the intelligent woman or the blue-stocking. I am interested in the girl who is not very brilliant, who takes her freedom with both hands and expresses it in the way that comes most naturally to her – particularly in her relations with men.

'Sometimes,' he added, 'because a girl is not very intelligent, things get out of hand and she finds that she can't always control the situation she has got herself into, or her emotions. As her approach is more direct and masculine her power over the man is necessarily diminished.'

Such was the Vadim philosophy in 1952, and less than eight years later, in the winter of 1960, he was able to summarise the realisation of his dream: 'People have attacked me because I have tried to show a girl of that kind achieving her own personal liberty. It can happen, of course, that when she has that liberty it's all too much for her, and that leads to drama and neurosis. I think that type of girl – the negligent, un-

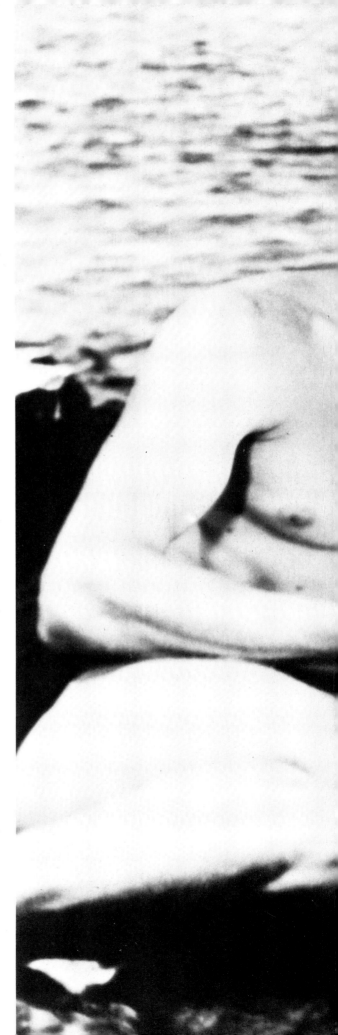

Brigitte playing 'an unclothed, wild little girl' in her first major part as *The Lighthouse Keeper's Daughter* (1952) with Jean-François Calvé

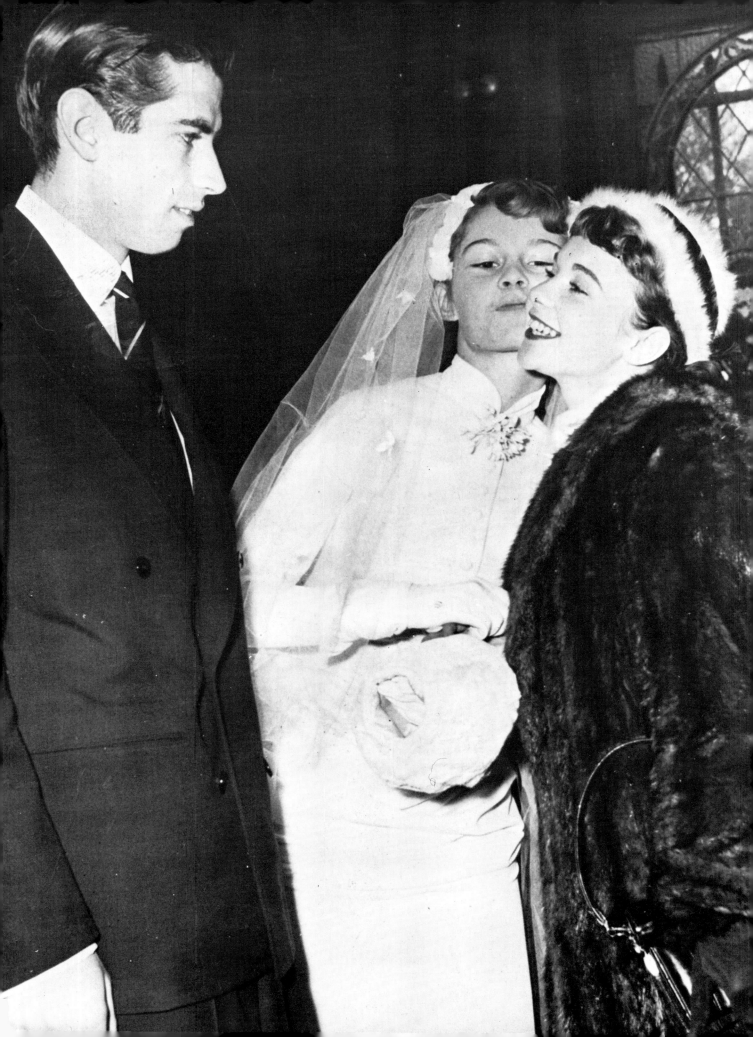

tidy hair, the tight skirt to show she is feminine, and the large pullover to show she wants to be comfortable – represents a certain category of women. I don't say it's the majority, but there are sufficient girls like that to make it a trend. It is surely the ideal way of showing femininity in an erotic manner. Much more exciting than spangles or ostrich feathers waving over the hips. It's more of a contrast than spangles, and it's the contrast which has the appeal. In other words, a woman who is slightly negligent or untidy is often more exciting than one who is dressed beautifully and faultlessly.'

Back in the spring of 1952, however, Vadim had no more than his dream – and a burning desire to get Brigitte into films. He spent many fruitless hours trying to inveigle film-makers in Paris into giving Brigitte a chance, until late in April he managed to get her a small part in Jean Boyer's film *Le Trou Normand* being made by Cite-Films in the village of Conches. Brigitte played a pretty young girl involved in a plot to deprive a rather weak-willed older man (played by the well-known French actor, Bourvil) from his inheritance of the village inn, *Le Trou Norman* (*The Norman Hole*). Brigitte was paid £300 for her fourteen days of acting on location during the middle two weeks of May.

Making her first film proved an unforgettable experience for the teenager – but not in the way she had expected. Because Vadim had spent so much time and energy on convincing her she *could* be a star, Brigitte desperately wanted to succeed for

his sake, if not her own. But, curiously, he had told her nothing at all about the mechanics of film-making. 'We started shooting without any hitches,' she recalled later. 'Everyone was kind enough to me, helping me over many difficulties and making what I did not like more agreeable. But as time went on I felt I was acting more and more badly – fantastically badly. I thought a film was made from the beginning to the end and not in disconnected little bits. I had thought that on the set I would be able to forget myself and my surroundings and give of my best. But it was nothing like that at all.

'I also did not like my part from the start – a little witch of a girl, somewhat vulgar, a little boorish and very sensual – but that, it seemed, was the star role of the picture and I was told by everybody that this was my big break. So you see film-making wasn't at all what I had expected. I felt let-down. Was it always to be like this? I wondered. I had my dream shattered. And the film was terrible.' (Although this subjective view by Brigitte may well be true, the film later became a great commercial success, re-titled *Crazy for Love*, earning several million dollars in America alone.)

Brigitte returned to Paris dejected and convinced that a career in films was not for her. But her love for Vadim quickly persuaded her to change her mind when he got her another film opportunity less than a month later. Just how much she was prepared to allow Vadim to guide her fortunes was evidenced by the fact that the new film, *Manina, La Fille Sans Voile* called for her to spend much of her time before the cameras in the following days of June and July in the skimpiest of bikinis.

The story of the film, re-titled for English-speaking audiences as *The Light-*

Brigitte and Roger Vadim photographed on their wedding day, 20 December 1952

house Keeper's Daughter, was set on the Corsican coast where two divers are trying to locate a sunken treasure ship. The simmering hostility between the two men boils over when the scantily-clad Brigitte appears on the scene. Her role required her to do little more than pose seductively – which she did superbly – but once again it proved highly unsatisfactory to Brigitte herself.

'I took the part of an unclothed, wild little girl as lacking in experience as the one in the first film,' she said in an interview a few years afterwards. 'My acting seemed even worse – later I used to blush with shame at the thought of it. I was just a cheap little starlet hardly acting at all in a very mediocre film.'

Somebody else who was less than pleased with Brigitte's role in *Manina* was her father. When word reached him about her scenes in the tiny bikini and one in which she appeared seemingly in the nude, he immediately called his lawyers and demanded to see a rough cut of the film. He was outraged by the near-naked appearance of his daughter and demanded that cuts be made before the film was released. Within hours the story of the angry father and his bikini-clad starlet daughter had made the pages of the French newspapers (almost certainly leaked to his friends in the press by Roger Vadim) and the film was well on its way towards generating considerable public interest even before it opened.

The film also provoked a personal crisis for Brigitte. Disillusioned by her two experiences before the cameras, she now begged Vadim to let her give up the idea of a film career. She would be eighteen in September, she said, why couldn't they get engaged and then be married, and she would be happy to settle down as a wife while he pursued his interests in the film industry without her.

The first wish was granted without further delay. Bardot *mère* and *père* saw it was pointless to keep the young lovers apart and agreed to an engagement on Brigitte's eighteenth birthday. Three months after this, on 20 December, the couple were married at the town hall on Avenue Henri Martin in the sixteenth arrondissement (consecrating the marriage the following day in the church of Notre-Dame de Grace in Auteil) and thereafter moved into a small flat in the Rue Chardon-Lagache, just around the corner from the Bardot family apartment.

Roger Vadim recalls that they were actually prevented from spending their first night together by Brigitte's father because their union had not been blessed by the church. 'I will leave you alone for ten minutes,' Louis Bardot had said. 'After that, Vadim, you will go to the dining room where I have made up a camp bed.' It was an unlikely beginning for the couple who were to herald the permissive era!

The second wish, however, met with the stiffest possible resistance from Vadim who was now more than ever sure that Brigitte *could* be a success as an actress. Already, he had sensed in *Manina* that his wife-to-be was moving towards the image of the 'new woman' he wanted to portray on the screen. Brigitte has told us how her change of heart was effected. 'Vadim changed my mind. Vadim was the only man who was certain I had something special to offer on the screen. I marvelled at his confidence and laughed at his conceit. It was difficult not to listen to his arguments.

'"As long as I am here," he told me, "you need never be afraid of people or of life. I shall guide you to success. I love you and will make you succeed." His trust gave

42

me fresh hope. I would do whatever he told me. He was both my teacher and master as well as my husband. I placed myself entirely in his hands. We went back to the beginning and he taught me how to speak, how to remember my lines, and tried to show me how to act. Love was the driving force. The experience improved and rewarded me.'

This love of Vadim's was to turn the hapless little starlet of *Crazy For Love* into one of the screen's great love objects, a woman who, in the starmaker's own words, was to become 'the unattainable dream of all respectable married men'.

Vadim spent hours watching and training his young wife to become a film actress

1953
Acts of Passion

THE NEWLYWEDS, MONSIEUR and Madame Plémiannikov, spent a brief honeymoon in the French alps that December of 1952, enjoying various winter sports (an activity Brigitte has continued to enjoy to this day, living for part of each winter in a chalet she owns at Meribel) and then returned to Paris where they set up their 'love nest' in the apartment in the Rue Chardon-Lagache.

Although the young couple made every effort to make their marriage work, in hindsight both accept that the traumas with Brigitte's parents and the generally unsettled state of their existence prior to their wedding day had affected both very deeply. Nonetheless, Brigitte devoted herself to all the tasks of a housewife – shopping, looking after the flat and struggling, unavailingly, to become a cook – while Vadim pursued his ambitions on the fringe of the film world and worked hard on new projects and scripts. Both feel that the year 1953 was basically a happy one, they were genuinely in love – but the portents of failure were soon to become evident.

Brigitte described that year in these words, 'Our love was so marvellous and so reciprocal. I used to wake up at night just so I could look at him. Little by little, though, the foundation of our love diminished. I was away from home much of the time – filming. At first I missed Vadim terribly. Later, I became used to our separations.'

Roger Vadim explained his own feelings with equal candour. 'Passion must last long enough to allow love to grow,' he says. 'If it dies too quickly, before there can be a marriage of souls, complete mutual understanding and the comfort of familiarity, the two people find themselves alone, driven by obscure desires and lost dreams. I see passion as a boat in which two people play and make love without noticing in their carefree happiness that there is a hole in the bottom. Their eyes are turned towards their destination, a beach holding out the promise of hot, white sand and shady trees. Day after day, week after week, the boat draws nearer the shore where they will live happily ever after, safe from the uncertainties of sea and weather. But the boat usually sinks before they reach the shore. 'For us, the boat trip had already lasted too long. The beach that Brigitte dreamed of was an impossible paradise. When the tide finally carried us ashore she didn't recognise it.'

A close observer of the relationship was, understandably enough, Brigitte's mother,

One of the photographs taken of Brigitte on the beach at Cannes which helped rocket her to stardom. This one has not previously been published

45

who only lived around the corner from the couple's flat. Shortly after their divorce, Mme Bardot spoke candidly about her daughter's marriage. 'Vadim was the very first man in her life,' she said. 'After all she was married at eighteen. She was really too young to realise what she wanted. I don't think there would ever have been a divorce, though, if he hadn't tried to make her into a kind of myth.

'My daughter is like a good-tempered bomb. You should see her when she visits us. She kisses everybody, including the maids and the dogs. She always has some funny story to tell us and acts it out until she has us all in stitches. She's not really temperamental, that's all false, and only on the surface. At heart she's still the little bourgeoise she always was.'

To illustrate this point, Mme Bardot recalls Brigitte arriving at her home one day and demanding, 'Mama, have you got the pink sheets from the laundry yet?' 'I said "Really, Brigitte, haven't you got anything else on your mind but sheets?"'

'I know my daughter. She loves life for all it brings her. And I thank heaven sometimes for the good sense that has always saved her at the last minute from making appalling blunders. Some of the things she says make her appear stupid. She isn't at all. She is a very shrewd little girl. The real Brigitte is a laughing happy girl full of practical jokes and enthusiasm.'

Turning to her daughter's husband, Mme Bardot was again candid, but showed no rancour or bitterness over what had happened. 'My ex-son-in-law is an odd fellow in many ways,' she said, 'but I have never been jealous of his influence over Brigitte. I admire his intelligence, but that has never stopped me from saying what I thought about him, or he about me, for that matter. Vadim has a tortured personality. He was brought up like that. There was always that difference between them. Brigitte tried very hard to turn herself into what he wanted because she was in love and was anxious to please.'

Just how anxious Brigitte was to please her husband was evidenced by the enthusiasm with which she now threw herself into moulding her personality into the one he dreamed of seeing projected on the cinema screen. In their little flat in the Rue Chardon-Lagache, under his guidance, she perfected the sexual pout, the fluttering eyelids, the provocative walk and complete lack of inhibition when undressing – all of which became her trademark. She recalls: 'Whenever I walked or undressed or ate breakfast, I always had the impression he was looking at me with someone else's eyes – and with everyone's eyes. Yet, I knew he was not seeing me, but through me, his dream.'

Away from the flat, Vadim dashed from film company to film company seeking parts for his wife: and not without success. In April he got her work at the Joinville Studios in her first joint French-American picture, *Quelque Part Dans La Monde*, released in English-speaking countries as *Act of Love*. Kirk Douglas was the star of this war-time love story featuring an American G.I. and a homeless French girl, and Brigitte later recalled that she was very nervous when she met the famous American actor on the set for the first time. His advice to her, though, was very encouraging, 'Take it easy. You'll make it. You'll get up there all right.'

These words from a much-respected professional were the first piece of genuine encouragement Brigitte had heard from anyone except her husband. They cheered the young actress greatly — even if a substantial part of her role as a maid in the hotel where the lovers stayed was cut from the finished film.

The following month Brigitte played a courtesan in Mondial Films' big-budget recreation of the story of Versailles, *If Versailles Could Talk*, which reunited her with the star of her very first film, Bourvil. A host of stars disported themselves in this grandiloquent, period-piece story — stars such as Sacha Guitry, Claudette Colbert, Orson Welles and Edith Piaf — and Brigitte's brief appearance carried no greater impact on audiences than that in *Act of Love*.

The end of May, however, saw the opening of the famed Cannes Film Festival and Vadim decided to gamble on an appearance there for Brigitte. He was sure if he could only put her on display at this traditional *fest* of hustling producers and hopeful starlets, her beauty, her stunning appearance when dressed in a bikini and, most of all, her so-obvious sexuality would make the world sit up and take notice. How right he was.

Skilfully, Vadim negotiated a place for his wife among the group of actors who had appeared in *Act of Love*, who were dispatched to Cannes to help promote the film. Although Brigitte's role had become so small as to be almost invisible, once at the festival she proceeded to make an even bigger impact than the real stars Kirk Douglas and Dany Robin. She achieved this impact in just the way Vadim always knew she would — by displaying her body. Strangely, however, it was to be an English journalist who first spotted and publicised the delightful young gamine laying on the Cannes beach. Leonard Mosley, veteran showbusiness writer of the *Daily Express*, is credited with having first publicised the girl who was destined to become the most famous headline-grabber of them all. Mosley had been attending the Film Festival for many years, and was rarely surprised by the publicity-inspired exploits of young starlets. Yet this girl whom he almost literally tripped over on the beach stopped him in his tracks.

'Brigitte Bardot was a strip of sunburned hoydenish girl lying on a Riviera beach and waiting for someone or something to turn up,' he says. 'I turned up. So did a *Daily Express* photographer who snapped her — lean, schoolgirl limbs, wasp-waist, adolescent bulges, long uncombed hair. This was Brigitte Bardot discovered!'

Mosley has written since in a reflective mood: 'At that moment in the minds of men something snapped. Until that time a woman had always been a woman, and looked it. Brigitte Bardot showed that woman could also look and act like a tomboy. Nothing phoney about her. She became the symbol to the world — through her films and through her private life — of the happy girl who leaves the other soppy females and goes down to play with the gang of boys on the street corner. The first of the beatniks — that was Bardot. If she failed to make an uncombed head and an unpowdered face acceptable, she at least made them seem attractive. Older women may have said that she always looked as if she needed a wash and brush-up; most men were apt to reply, "What does soap matter as long as she's friendly?" Bardot ushered in the era of the great unmade bed. And from the beaches of St. Tropez to the gang-infested alleyways of backstreet New York, she became the imaginary champion of females who accepted her looks and her attitudes as a way of life.'

Leonard Mosley closed his first report on that May morning in 1953 with the words, 'Watch what happens to this French girl Brigitte Bardot.'

Vadim, however, wanted Brigitte to capture the attention of more than just one English reporter and photographer. When the US Navy Aircraft Carrier *Midway* arrived off Cannes to play customary host to all the stars, he slipped her aboard demurely – and seemingly unsuitably – dressed in a raincoat. A colleague on the magazine *Paris Match*, which Vadim had recently quit, but had undoubtedly tipped the wink as to what was going to happen, chronicled the event:

'Then the girl in the raincoat caught the photographers' eyes. The raincoat slipped from her shoulders. She emerged in a tight-fitting teenager's dress and with a toss of her head sent her ponytail flying. There was a second of silence, just enough for the electric charge to pass between the crowd of males and the figure in the floodlights. Then the *Midway* was engulfed in a single shot of lightning and a crash of thunder: thousands of flashbulbs and shouts of admiration that exceeded in volume all the previous acclaims put together.'

Roger Vadim, not far away as this extraordinary unveiling occurred, was already dreaming up his press quotes. 'She is a photographic phenomenon,' he was to say later. 'Most of her success is due to the fact that she is one hundred per cent photogenic.' Not a single man – or woman – who was on the *Midway* that May day would have argued with that statement.

And while she revelled in the attention, Brigitte herself knew that something else irrevocably had happened to her. 'Vadim,' she said, 'had at last released me from my bourgeois prison.'

Madeira
METROPOLE KINE
RAVEX
LE TRAIN AVEC UN
00022
de FAMILLE
PECIAL
TUFI PAZ

1954
Three in a Bed

ALL THE PIN-UP shots which Brigitte had attracted at Cannes and which quickly found their way into magazines and newspapers – principally in Europe – understandably earned her more attention in film circles, and Vadim found it easier to obtain new parts for her. Not, though, that she had yet made any kind of real impact on the screen.

Early in the spring of 1954 she once again left the flat in the Rue Chardon-Lagache for the film studios. This time, however, it was not a French, or even joint production, but an epic spectacle being shot in Rome by Warner Brothers. The six-million-dollar film was *Helen of Troy*, and though Brigitte might well have made an excellent Helen (the part was actually taken by the Italian star Rosanna Podesta) she was actually cast as the Queen's handmaiden, Andraste. The picture was expected to be a great spectacular. It was being filmed in colour, had the prestigious director Robert Wise in charge, and was weighed down with both British and American film stars. Not surprisingly, Brigitte and Vadim travelled to Rome full of high hopes.

All Rome was astir about the picture when they arrived. Stories of the huge number of people being employed in its production, as well as accounts of the enormous sets being built to stage the wars between Troy and Greece, not to mention the gigantic Wooden Horse, were on everyone's lips. Despite the fact that Brigitte came to the Roman capital highly vaunted because of her achievement at Cannes – the film world has always been ready to embrace the star capable of achieving really big media coverage – she and Vadim had to settle for staying at one of the smaller hotels in the city. Still, her reputation had gone before her and Rome's notorious photographers, the *paparazzi*, were waiting to catch her every movement. In these early years of her career she did not disappoint them: later, as a major star, they were to be the bane of her life.

Work on the film proved hardly taxing for Brigitte, and Vadim remembered the stay more for an incident which was to become part of his legend when he was later labelled as a cynical, shameless hedonist – 'that Devil Vadim' as he was called – who exploited the bodies of his various wives across the cinema screens of the world. Vadim has recounted the incident in his own words:

'We were in the Rome of the *dolce vita*. Ursula Andress had run away from her boarding school in Switzerland to be with Daniel Gélin, for whom she had lost her seventeen-year-old head and her innocence. After a few hectic weeks (one needed a stout constitution to keep up with the

51

frenzied pace of life with Daniel) the grand passion began to wilt. Ursula came to seek refuge in our hotel room. We only had one double bed, and as the weather was very hot, Brigitte, Ursula and I slept in the nude.

'In the morning we breakfasted out on the sunlit balcony overlooking the seven hills, Brigitte and Ursula leant laughing, suntanned and naked over the balcony to throw bread crusts down onto passers-by in the Via Sistina. It was delightful to behold, and I wonder how many saints would have been safe from eternal damnation had they found themselves in my position? And yet I did not allow myself one little kiss. During the weeks Ursula spent with us, the innocent gaiety of our *ménage à trois* was not marred by the slightest dubious gesture. To be candid, it was not for lack of inclination, but I knew that Brigitte would not have appreciated fraternisation of that nature, so the Devil wore his halo to bed!'*

As this incident clearly demonstrates, Brigitte had now thrown off most of her bourgeois inhibitions, and was ready to exhibit her body as freely before the cameras as she had done on that hotel balcony. Vadim's hours of teaching and guidance had brought her to the verge of achieving the image he wanted for her. There can

* Vadim has also written in his autobiography that, 'Brigitte and Ursula loved to be told fantastic stories. In bed I would spin them tales about vampires, succubi and incubi. They squealed and hid under the sheets.' As a man who 'adored the fantastic' – to quote his own words – it was perhaps not surprising that Roger Vadim later compiled his own book of vampire stories, *I Vampiri tra Noi* published in Italy in 1960 and later translated into English in 1963 where it enjoyed considerable success under the simpler title of *The Vampire*. He also adapted one of the stories from the book, 'Carmilla' by Joseph Sheridan Le Fanu as the basis for his film *Et Mourir de Plaisir* made in 1970.

be little doubt that by then, he was well aware that he was on the verge of success – he just needed the role in which the beautiful, sexy butterfly could take wing.

This exhibitionist side of Brigitte's nature has intrigued many who have written about her life, and led to a much more likely explanation of her relationship with Vadim than the one fostered for so many years that it was he who 'created' her, nudity and all. Personality writer, Willi Frischauer has best put it into words:

'The received wisdom among analysts of the Bardot phenomenon is that Vadim exploited her body for professional purposes and incited her to orgies of nudity on the screen as if he had unfrocked an unwilling victim. But Brigitte's own exhibitionism has been played down. Very frequently it was she who was anxious to show off her stunning physical assets. Vadim could only be blamed because what happened – or did not happen – between them at home intensified their quest to find satisfaction elsewhere. It was not so much a matter of Vadim, the Devil, leading her astray, as of Brigitte, the Eve, forever offering the apple of temptation to all who cared to take a bite.'

With two such personalities joined in wedlock, it comes as no surprise to learn that by the summer of 1954, their marriage was in trouble. Certainly they rowed and made up, but Vadim would let nothing stand in the way of his dream. Brigitte herself recalls of this period of her life: 'We worked – how we worked! Gradually I overcame my fear, I played more parts, better parts, even if they were smaller parts in other people's films.'

Late in June, Brigitte was back in France working on location at Roussillon and later in the Studios Saint-Maurice in Paris on *Le*

Fils de Caroline Cherie. Now, with Vadim's teaching having firmly established her style and with her earlier experiences behind her, she approached this new project for the first time with real confidence. From her first appearance on the screen, it was evident that here was a more polished and self-assured actress. The film was actually the third in a series, built around a character named Caroline Cherie, created in the novels of Cécil Saint-Laurent. In the two previous movies, the title role had been taken by the beautiful Martine Carol. Brigitte, though, was determined not to fall under her shadow, and stamped her own very special personality on Pilar, the young Spanish girl who romances with handsome Jean-Claude Pascal, 'The Son of Caroline Cherie'. A costume drama, set during the French occupation of Spain, the film was to gain the young actress some of her first – and complimentary – reviews when it appeared.

There was to be a strange twist of fate about the third film Brigitte made in 1954, once again shot in the Studios Saint-Maurice. It brought together the rapidly-developing young star and the man who had first spotted her potential on the cover of *Elle* but then decided against filming her – Marc Allegret. There can be little doubt that Roger Vadim had remained in close contact with his mentor while he was building Brigitte into a star, and doubtless told him about each of her films. Then, in the autumn of 1954, he finally convinced Allegret that his wife could now act, and the three of them began work on a joint project. The film was *Futures Vedettes* based on a novel by Vicki Baum, and both Vadim and Allegret worked on the screen treatment. Brigitte, too, played her part, becoming closely involved in the writing of the dia-

Vadim and Bardot in Rome together in the spring of 1954

logue. As Vadim explains: 'She spoke and I wrote. The words in that film, as in a number of our films together, are really hers. They are written for her, because she more or less wrote them.'

Filming began on 10 December, and Allegret coaxed another good performance out of Brigitte as a besotted music student in love with a much older opera singer, played by Jean Marais. A nice touch about the film was that in it Vadim gave Brigitte the nickname they enjoyed in private: Sophie. The sensual love scenes and the nude sequence seem in retrospect clear forerunners of the major films which were now just around the corner.

During the making of this picture – later retitled with notable incongruity *Sweet Sixteen* – during the winter of 1954–5, Vadim began to nurse hopes that Brigitte might perhaps catch the eye of an American film company. She had some experience with people from the Mecca of the film world in pictures like *Act of Love* and *Helen of Troy*, and he knew that if he was going to make her a famous household name, she needed a Hollywood vehicle to get her real international exposure.

In fact *Futures Vedettes* did catch the eye of some foreign film-makers – but not from across the Atlantic, as Vadim hoped. Rather, from across the much shorter distance of the English Channel where a well-established partnership was looking for a girl to cast in a nautical comedy they were about to begin shooting. At first sight, the sensual French gamine Brigitte Bardot might have seemed oceans away from what was needed in a light-hearted English picture. But the producer, Betty Box, and director, Ralph Thomas, had sensed something rather special about Brigitte, both from her film appearances (brief though they mainly were) and multitudinous pin-ups in Continental magazines and papers, and wanted to give her a try.

It was to prove an inspired piece of casting from their point of view – and was to give Brigitte her second taste of film-making abroad. The picture was also to make her for the first time a household name – 'The Sex Kitten' to be precise – in the unexpected surroundings of normally oh-so-sedate Great Britain . . .

A previously unpublished still of Brigitte from *Helen of Troy*: the film in which she might have been the star

1955
The Sex Kitten Appears

BRIGITTE ARRIVED IN London to film her part in the Rank Organisation's picture *Doctor at Sea* in March. Although she had no reputation in Britain as yet, her stunning good looks and unashamed sexuality made an instant impact on all who saw her. Co-star in the film, Dirk Bogarde, who kept a diary of the making of the picture which was published in *Picturegoer* magazine, commented in an entry for 19 March 1955: 'She has a superb figure, long legs, flowing hair and gazelle-like grace.'

The producer of the film, Betty Box, had become aware of Brigitte's growing appeal through the careful eye she always kept on Continental films. Then, when the English actress Kay Kendall (star of the very popular *Genevieve*) turned down the part of the young cabaret singer in the film about a doctor's antics on a cargo-steamer en route for South America, she decided to plump for the young French starlet. Brigitte did not let her down in either her acting or the publicity she generated.

The director of the film, Ralph Thomas, was also quickly captivated by Brigitte once she appeared on the set at Pinewood. But such was her impact on the place as a whole that he soon found work almost impossible as people made any excuse to sneak a look at her. 'For weeks all the men in the studio were going around with cricks

in their necks,' Thomas recalls. 'She really has the most fabulous legs.'

During the course of the making of *Doctor at Sea*, Brigitte pulled another of the strokes which helped create her legend. In one sequence she had to be disturbed by Dirk Bogarde while she was in a shower. Initially it was planned to shoot the scene with Brigitte behind the shower curtain, her modesty protected by bikini pants and nipple covers. But no matter how the set was lit, the camera still picked up the outline of these garments and made the scene ludicrous.

While Betty Box, Ralph Thomas and the cameraman pondered the problem, Brigitte solved it for them. She calmly strip-

ped off all her clothes and presented herself *au naturale* before the open-mouthed crew. The scene was shot without further delay – and by the end of the day the young French actress was the centre of gossip all over Pinewood. The rest of the world would hear soon after. As film critic Tony Crawley has said of this scene 'Daring it was; and even if no more flesh than a shoulder and her lately-labelled Pekinese face were to be seen peeking around the shower curtain, it probably constituted the first naked actress in a British film studio.'

Bogarde also noted in his diary for *Picturegoer*, 'She was like a breath of Oklahoma on the set every day. The kind of sex she suggests is warm, uninhibited, completely natural . . . You see, Brigitte takes the trouble to put across sex as an art. With many of our girls, it's a farce.'

It was quite evident from reports such as this that Brigitte had learned all the lessons her husband had taught her. But when news of the impact she was having reached Vadim in Paris, where he had been kept working on another film script, he was naturally delighted at the response – but quite amazed that it should have been the British who first really appreciated her unique screen quality.

Later he explained what he believed to be the secret of her appeal, an explanation that anyone who has met Brigitte in the intervening years will agree still holds good today: 'Brigitte's secret is the impact she has on people. You know, there is a certain kind of person who arrives in a room and you don't know for what reason – you are

Brigitte meets Dirk Bogarde – he was very impressed with his French co-star in *Doctor at Sea*

58

59

talking to someone else, maybe – but you feel this presence and you have to turn your head and watch this person. Maybe to criticise, maybe to compliment. But you *have* to turn and watch. Brigitte had this kind of quality. A real break with the tradition of the actress at this time. It did not mean she was a great actress – her style was quite different. And totally natural.'

The mountains of press cuttings which reached him from British newspapers and magazines – front-page stories mixed with pin-up pictures galore – were the most substantial his wife had ever attracted: swamping even those which she had drawn at the Cannes Film Festival. Vadim knew in that moment that Brigitte had arrived, and to this day he pays full credit to what happened across the Channel: 'The British first really saw her talent – even if it was only as a piece of French spiciness. When she went to London she was hardly known outside of France. In London a crowd of photographers came along to take pictures and almost every paper in England carried a pin-up type picture of her the following day.'

Though several newspapers and magazines can take some credit for this promotion of the Bardot image *Picturegoer* magazine certainly deserves a lion's share of the credit. Apart from publishing Dirk Bogarde's diary of the making of the picture (something of an unusual exercise in those days), it also carried a serialisation of the picture which again bore Bogarde's name as author. These items, plus several cover photographs of Bardot, and a number of articles by one of the magazine's star writers, Derek Walker, thrust her name and voluptuous features before millions of readers.

Particularly noteworthy among these contributions was Derek Walker's article which demanded in three-inch high letters, 'Is She The Hottest Glamour Tip Yet?' He began the piece, 'I read that, according to a normally quite sedate British publicist, she "combines sensuality with candour . . . reads the classics, yet swears like a trooper . . . in a few short months has outstripped her rivals in the world glamour stakes," So I just *had* to find out.'

As one of the earliest substantial features in which Bardot is quoted directly, Walker's item is important in the build-up of the legend as well as throwing an interesting light on her attitude towards the press at this crucial moment in her career. This is how Walker continues his story: 'This girl who has created such a fuss is known by many pet names. The Gorgeous Pekinese, for instance. And the Little Gazelle, Little Miss Innocent and, most recently, The Sex Kitten. I wondered which of these varied names would best fit Miss Brigitte Bardot.'

Walker talked to her while she curled up on a sofa, 'showing her big, bright teeth and making a sound halfway between a human giggle and a kittenish purr.' She was wearing a tight-bodiced dress that 'began well below the neck and ended at the white of a frilly petticoat halfway down her calves.' Here, indeed, he said, was The Sex Kitten. The report continues: 'I showed her the British publicist's quote and asked whether it was an apt summing up. "Yes," she said. "It is." Not the person she plays on the screen? – "There is no difference. I cannot separate myself from my movie characters. We are usually the same." As almost all her film roles are those of slinky, siren-like little creatures who know just how to catch a masculine man this was a startling admission.

'So she can swear like a trooper? "Yes" But *does* she swear like a trooper? "No." Does she really read the classics? "A little." Does she like being called The Sex Kitten and having hundreds of pin-up pictures taken of her? She giggled, smoothed her dress over her thighs, tweaked the lock of long corn-gold hair that twirled over her shoulder. "It is" she said, "nice. But I want to be an actress, too." This began to sound like the old story: get all the publicity you can, in bikinis on the beach, then switch to a sou-wester and shapeless mac and call yourself an actress. "However," continued Miss Bardot, haltingly, "being a good actress is a bore. And I am not a good actress. I would like to dance the ballet also . . . like Leslie Caron." But if she had to decide, one or the other? Miss Bardot did not hesitate for a second: "I'd be sexy." This was The Sex Kitten speaking, with the sort of candour that would shake Pinewood to its foundations and bring a blush even to the cheeks of Hollywood. Brigitte Bardot *likes* making love on the screen.

'She is soon to be directed in a film by her husband. (Her married name is Plémiannikov). Will this worry her in the love scenes? No, she says, there is an understanding, a rapport, that will help the scenes along. "We are," she says, "very much in love."

'Just what does all this add up to? A glamour star – not just a pin-up picture? Not quite, but it's early days. But I say this: to the Continental names that have worldwide meaning – Michèle Morgan, Martine Carol, La Lollo, Loren – add Brigitte Bardot. So far she's only a shape, a pet name and the sort of funny, big-eyed face you're not sure is beautiful. Give her time, a year or two . . . maybe she *is* the hottest glamour tip yet.'

There is also an interesting and prophetic footnote to Derek Walker's piece. He added that Brigitte's big ambition at that moment was to play the lead in a proposed British film called *Manuela* in which a girl disguises herself as a boy, joins the all-male crew of a ship and is discovered. Walker saw this as 'some situation for The Sex Kitten!' – but time has shown it as an uncannily accurate prophecy in both format and title of the notorious Emanuelle films of the 1970s. Unconsciously, even then, Brigitte was generating the climate for much greater freedom in portraying sex on the screen.

When Brigitte returned to France in early April, she found Vadim had been busy in her absence. Though their love might now have cooled – despite her press statements to the contrary – he had not spared himself in his efforts to get her more screen roles. And with news of her success in England having gone before her, this did not prove difficult. By 28 April, she was in residence at the Studios Boulogne for three months work on *Les Grandes Manoeuvres* (retitled *Summer Manoeuvres*). Directed by René Clair and co-starring Gerard Phillipe and Michèle Morgan, Brigitte played a pretty young flirt amongst a garrison of soldiers. Something of a contrast to her previous films, it did give Brigitte the chance of working with a great director on a film he was later to consider among his favourites.

From *Summer Manoeuvres*, she went straight into a role much closer to her Vadim-inspired *persona*. This was *La Lumiere D'en Face* (suggestively retitled for the English-language markets *The Light Across The Street*) in which she played a sensual young child-bride saddled with an impotent husband and attracted towards a virile neighbour. It was typical of several films then being made in France, but had something they all lacked – Brigitte at her most erotic. Although it was accepted and widely praised in the country of its creation, it ran swiftly into trouble when it crossed the Channel. Brigitte's scenes in which she flaunted her body before the two men, washed and preened herself, only too aware she was being observed, and then bathed naked in a river, brought the wrath of the censors down on it. In several parts of the country, *The Light Across The Street* was banned, in others extensive cuts were required. This was to prove just the first of Brigitte's many brushes with narrow-minded public bodies – although the controversy and headlines did no harm whatsoever to her developing legend. The picture has, with justification, been described as 'her first most definite erotica', and Vadim added to this his comment that it was 'popular in the way people today will go to see a pornographic movie'.

Brigitte finished off this hectic but important year filming a sexy comedy entitled *Cette Sacrée Gamine* (alternatively retitled *Mam'selle Pigalle* or *That Crazy Kid*) in which she had further scope for some voluptuous undressing as well as demonstrating for the first time on the screen her undoubted ability as a dancer. One can see clearly from this picture that she would have made a very polished dancer had she chosen that profession instead of acting.

Vadim had co-written the script for this picture, and his touch is evident both in some of Brigitte's lines and her nude or near-nude sequences. It was almost as if he was putting the finishing touches to his 'new woman' in preparation for her real unveiling. . . .

Brigitte upstaged in her 1955 film *Mam'zelle Pigalle*. It was rarely to happen again

62

1956
'And the World Discovered BB!'

THE YEAR 1956 began in a whirl of activity for Brigitte Bardot. First there was a return trip to Rome to film another costume spectacular, *Mio Figlio Nerone* (retitled *Nero's Weekend*) in which she played Poppea, mistress to Alberto Sordi's Nero. The picture was light-hearted, funny and showed off Brigitte in a variety of revealing costumes, as well as offering a bathing scene for which she garnered a lot of publicity by insisting that the pool be filled with asses's milk as the historical original had been! Brigitte also had the chance of acting with one of the *grand dames* of the cinema, Gloria Swanson, who played the Emperor's troublesome mother, Agrippina.

On 13 February, Brigitte travelled to Paris to work at the Studios Eclair on another joint venture between her husband and his mentor, Marc Allegret, *En Effeuillant La Marguerite*, (rather absurdly retitled later *Mam'zelle Striptease*). Starring opposite Vadim's old friend, Daniel Gélin, she made the most of the part of a young bourgeois beauty who is thrown out of her home for

Brigitte in the film which was to make her world-famous, *And God Created Woman*

writing a scandalous, best-selling book. Unwittingly drawn into breaking the law, she has to take part in a striptease contest – disguised behind a mask – to raise the money to cover up her crime. When the mask comes off, the faces of the onlookers are red for more reasons than one.

There were certain elements in the story which clearly harked back to Brigitte's earlier life, particularly her relationship with her screen parents, but there were no parental protests. The only cries of outrage which greeted the picture came from Italy, where it was denounced as 'offensive and immoral'. The Italian distributors had apparently re-titled the picture *Miss Spogliarello*, and depicted Brigitte in various stages of her striptease on the advertising posters. Outraged citizens proceeded to rip these from the walls wherever they appeared. In France, though, they had the last laugh when the film-makers, EGE/Hoch Productions issued a new poster which showed the Italian poster being ripped from a wall. *Plucking The Daisy* proved a most appropriate title for this picture in more ways than one.

Amidst all this frenzy of work, neither Brigitte nor Roger Vadim realised that they were about to confront their moment of destiny. That spring, Vadim had met another young film-maker in Paris and their immediate liking for each other had lead to the creation of a joint project. The man's name was Raoul Levy, and Vadim later described him as a person 'who tossed a thousand ideas around in his head . . . masochistic and tyrannical, attractive and repulsive, he had a genius for making people forgive him for everything . . . I cursed him a thousand times and loved him faithfully.'

This is how Vadim has described the birth of their venture. 'Even before we had decided what the film was going to be about we announced that Brigitte Bardot would play the lead, which didn't help matters. The stars of the day were Michèle Morgan, Martine Carole, Dany Robin and Françoise Arnoul. Nevertheless, Raoul found a producer who had confidence in my potential as a director. His name was Ray Ventura. Famous before the war for his college boys' band, Ray was brilliantly successful in the cinema. And in agreeing to co-produce our film (which did not yet even have a title) he displayed flair and courage. As far as the screenplay was concerned I knew what I wanted to say, but I needed a plot. One day Raoul Levy mentioned a recent news item: three brothers, a village, a beautiful woman, a crime – and . . . *Et Dieu Créa la Femme* was born.'

Raoul Levy has also explained how the project came to fruition, speaking in his typically abrupt style not long after the film was released in 1958: 'What happened was a sheer accident. You can't set out to create someone like Brigitte Bardot intentionally. It just happens when the time is right. It was like this. I had a contract with a script-

The unveiling of BB: In *Mam'zelle Striptease* (1956), Brigitte decides to enter a striptease contest to earn some much needed money

writer named Roger Vadim who happened to have a wife named Brigitte Bardot whom nobody was taking seriously. We wrote a film together, *And God Created Woman*, which was a basically bad script but honest in its observation of how people lived on the French Riviera. Well, we couldn't get anyone to finance Vadim, Brigitte and me. We were three failures nobody wanted to know. Then we persuaded Curt Jurgens to appear in the film and once we had him we were able to get the finance. It cost £150,000 and it will gross £3,000,000.'

Levy has also expressed his opinions on Brigitte's appeal. 'It is in the mind of the audience,' he says. 'It is not what she shows that counts. It is what they think they can see. And they are always one jump ahead of us in that respect.' True to a degree though this statement is, it was the firm intention of the Vadim-Levy partnership to show absolutely as much as possible of Brigitte Bardot in *And God Created Woman*.

Once the services of Curt Jurgens had been safely secured, the two men could get down to the fine details of their idea. Although such catch-phrases as the 'permissive society' and 'women's liberation' had not yet been coined, what they had in mind was very close to those later ideals, as Vadim has explained about the film which was to mark his debut as a director. 'I wanted, through Brigitte, to witness an epoch,' he said, 'the psychosis of our post-war generation. Juliette (played by Brigitte) is a young girl of today, to whom the taste of pleasure is neither limited by morals or social taboos; entirely free in her sexual behaviour. In pre-war literature and cinema one would have painted her simply as a whore. Here she is a very young woman without, of course, any excuses save for those of the heart, of a generous, inconsist-ent person.'

The film was shot primarily on the beach at St. Tropez (then unknown as a playground for the rich), and there amidst a welter of surf, sand and hot sun, Brigitte played out her role of the sexually precocious young girl seducing three young brothers and a wealthy shipping magnate (played by Jurgens). 'That girl can drive men wild,' one of the characters was made to say in the jointly written lines by Vadim and Levy – and that, in truth, was to be Brigitte's impact on audiences around the world when the film was released. As Tony Crawley said: 'The film that created the myth, the actress who wasn't an actress but herself, as amoral, Vadim said, Bardot said, as Juliette on the screen. The film that hardly bothered the French and shook up the rest of the globe and changed the face of the cinema.'

Vadim himself worked on the picture with the sure hand of a man who knew exactly what he was doing. He had carefully nurtured Brigitte for this moment; harnessed her energy, her sensuality and her beauty to make a profound, an important, and equally, a commercially successful film. When he published his autobiography, *Memoirs of the Devil* in 1975, he paid tribute to the importance of this film in his life on the very first page: 'Despite one or two cuts (which would make a schoolgirl smile indulgently today) Brigitte Bardot was delivered unveiled and free of bourgeois taboos to the public. She was to cross national borders to give the world a foretaste of a new morality. In her inimitably shameless manner she flouted the Ten Commandments by demonstrating that sex was no longer a sin. There was nothing diabolical about this explosion of pagan candour, but something had been started:

the posters proclaimed that "Woman was created by God and BB was invented by the Devil". The nickname has stuck to me ever since.'

However, all the sensation which was to result from *And God Created Woman* was still some months away, and once work at St. Tropez and in the studios at Nice was over, Brigitte returned to Paris to make a previously contracted film, *La Mariée est trop Belle* (*The Bride Is Too Beautiful*). This story of a young village beauty turned into a legend by way of magazine covers contained some of the elements of her own life. And if she had foreseen the impact of the film she had just completed in the South of France, she would have known that like Chouchou in the picture, her face, style and manners were also going to be copied by young girls everywhere. Instead Brigitte summed-up the film afterwards, 'I find it a bit silly.' And that also proved to be the view of the public when it was released.

One critical development from filming *And God Created Woman*, was Brigitte's affair with her leading man, Jean-Louis Trintignant, the brother with whom she finally settles. Although apparently unimpressed with the dark, rather sombre-looking Trintignant when she first met him, Brigitte had fallen in love with him by the end of the picture, and this led to the parting of the ways for her and the man who had, as she said, 'released me from my bourgeois prison'.

The break did not come as a surprise to Vadim and he later spoke of it with cool, if somewhat colourful, objectivity. 'I had not expected it to be Jean-Louis Trintignant,' he said, 'but I had been preparing myself for this moment for over a year. Now I

Brigitte with Curt Jurgens who made possible the filming of *And God Created Woman*

wanted our first film to take the place of the child we had not had. I wanted it to be the seed and the fruit of seven years of tumult and hope. The parting of the ways rather than the end of the road.' The passage of time has seen that expression amply fulfilled – Brigitte and Roger Vadim have remained close friends, seeking each other's counsel frequently, still sharing their memories of a unique partnership.

A month before the opening of *And God Created Woman* in Paris, Brigitte received confirmation of her status as a star – if such she needed – when she was invited to be a guest at the Royal Command Film Performance in London. Meeting the Queen proved a memorable occasion – as did her brief encounter with the world's current number one sex symbol, Marilyn Monroe.

Brigitte was evidently in good spirits during this London trip, for her press conference on 3 November was full of charm and flashes of wit, and she also came across well in a personal interview given later to that perceptive doyen of British show-business writers, Logan Gourley. He also managed to prise rather more out of her about her philosophy of life than English readers had enjoyed previously. Gourley prefaced his interview with a note that 'Miss Bardot speaks a brand of fractured English which makes her sound at times like the French maid in a bad bedroom farce' – but admitted he found it rather delightful and advised her not to learn English too well. This is how his report went on:

'Miss Bardot has quite an effect on people, particularly men. I had noticed at her press reception a few hours earlier that normally intelligent, articulate men were struck dumb in her presence or reduced to banality. One asked her what she thought of London policemen. Another – an influential editor – stared at her as though mesmerised and about to leap through her outsized hoop earrings. Then he swallowed and asked what perfume she was wearing. She replied: "Mouche" and gazed abstractedly at herself in the mirror behind him. She looked as usual like a girl who has stepped out of an ad. for corsetry and put a dress on (hurriedly).

'Now in the mouche-scented bedroom of her Savoy Hotel suite, as Miss Bardot gazed into another mirror, I shook off the spell and asked her if she was embarrassed by the stares and reactions of men she encountered.

'"No, no, of course not. I am flattered. I would be sad if the men paid no attention to me." I told her that an intellectual young lady had said – a little enviously – at the Press reception, "She has an air of innocent depravity – and she probably doesn't know what depravity means." Miss Bardot said: "It is something to do with sin, isn't it? I know what sin is." (She sounded like a child talking about a toy.) "People are always saying and writing funny things about me."

'I showed her a copy of an article about her written by Roger Vadim which said among other things that "In order of preference after Clown, her pet spaniel, she likes other dogs, birds, money, Empire furniture, kittens and baby monkeys. I probably come in between the kittens and the monkeys." Miss Bardot laughed loudly at the last line. She is now separated from her husband. "Why did I separate? Why? It is simple," she said, making me feel like a father who has raised what his daughter considers a rather silly question. "I fell in love with another man. That is why. He is an actor. He appears with me in my latest film.'' (Her husband directed it.) ''Are you going to get a divorce and marry again?'' ''Divorce, maybe. But never marry again. I married when I was too young – only eighteen. Now I am older and wiser.'' (She is a ripe twenty-two.) ''I do not like marriage. Always one man. I want to be free.'' ''What type of man do you prefer?'' ''Many types. I do not care very much how they look. Except for the mouth. I like a man who has a big mouth. It shows he is generous,'' she added with an earring-to-earring smile. ''But he doesn't have to be rich. I like money to spend but I never worry about it.''

'I said that, according to her husband, she had a serious-minded interest in modern philosophy and Existentialism. ''Nonsense, I know nothing about these things. Nothing. I am not clever. I am silly.''

'Cleverly silly, I'd say. A contradiction in curves like that other depraved innocent or naive seductress Marilyn Monroe. A walking – wiggling – paradox.'

Within a few days of making those remarks, the 'walking – wiggling – paradox' that was Brigitte Bardot was to be unveiled as a true 'Goddess of the Screen' and earn a reputation that has survived to this day. . . .

A famous still from *And God Created Woman*

1957
A New Sex Appeal

ET DIEU CRÉA LA FEMME had its world première at the Normandie Cinema in the Champs-Élysées on the evening of 4 December 1956 and was greeted with almost unanimously hostile reviews in the French press. Vadim, though naturally disappointed, consoled himself with the fact that there were so many contradictions in the reviews – brought about, he thought, by the journalists' differing views on politics, morality and religion – that perhaps others elsewhere might see his work differently. He could not believe he had put so much of his life and thoughts into a film for it to be all wrong.

As soon as the picture, first retitled *And Woman . . . Was Created*, and later *And God Created Woman*, was screened outside France, throughout the rest of Europe, and then in America, Vadim was triumphantly vindicated. During the twelve months of 1957 Bardot and her steamy, erotic, visually exciting picture became one of the most talked-about subjects in the western world (and many points beyond).

In London the critics were left open-mouthed in amazement. 'I'm prepared to bet an overcoat to a bikini that this film will make its star Miss Sex of the Universe,' wrote Matt White of the tabloid *Daily Sketch*. 'In a lifetime of seeing movies, I have never seen an actress convey sex so simply

and so devastatingly. . . . She had me blushing in the nervous darkness of the cinema.' The more up-market *Daily Mail*'s critic, Cecil Wilson, also enthused, 'Censored or uncensored, this actress has a way of making her meaning clear. But if her performance consists largely of a smouldering pout, it must be remembered that Mlle Bardot can smoulder to better purpose than most other screen sirens can blaze.' Donald Zec, of the *Daily Mirror*, who had actually seen some of the filming being done while he was in the South of France, could only gasp, 'It's the most flagrant, suggestive, near the knuckle picture I have ever seen anywhere.'

After the film had opened throughout Europe it transpired that Vadim had had to fight hard with the French censor who wanted a number of cuts made – particularly in the love-making scenes between Brigitte and Jean-Louis Trintignant (who were, by this time, really in love with each other). The *French* censor, indeed! But Vadim was persistent. He was determined to preserve the meaning of his film, and by so doing he retained the dimension he wanted, and helped it immensely in its later tremendous success at the box office. In London, however, the British Censor proved more lenient, and it was passed with an 'X' certificate which made it accessible to all audiences over the age of sixteen.

It was not until October that the picture opened in New York, heralded with an enormous poster of Brigitte, semi-naked, dominating busy Time Square. But its impact there was even greater than anywhere else, as French journalist Renaud de Laborderie, who produced the first in-depth study of the BB phenomenon, reported in 1964: 'Leaving for New York with the reels of film in his suitcase, Raoul Levy, who had bought his air ticket by scraping together all his savings, had one ambition: to exploit for the best price the sexy appeal of Brigitte Bardot, with whom he had signed a contract for four further films, and to sell *And God Created Woman* as quickly as possible. His sole preoccupation was to restore his finances which had been rendered precarious by his meagre career in French commercial films. In reality, he introduced dynamite into the United States.

'It was a typhoon, a floodtide, an atomic explosion! Within a few days the name of Brigitte Bardot swept the American continent from coast to coast at lightning speed. Incidents followed in quick succession and bans of all kinds ensued. Preachers fulminated against the film from the pulpit; the censors tried to prevent it being shown, in the Puritan states a few cinema managers were flung in jail; the watch committees staged protest meetings . . . and all this hullabaloo brought the film an unprecedented success.

'In a host of towns including San Francisco, Chicago, Detroit and Philadelphia, *And God Created Woman* exceeded the fabulous receipts of Cecil B. de Mille's *Ten Commandments*. Within three months Brigitte Bardot had become the No. 1 foreign star in the USA. She had brought to the Americans a new sex appeal, very different from the sophisticated, hypocritical sex appeal of Hollywood. By osmosis her fame extended throughout the world like a flow of lava from a volcano in eruption. In Tokyo as in Buenos Aires, in Stockholm as in Hong Kong, in Johannesburg as in Berlin, *And God Created Woman* defeated every ban, flouted the puritan spirits and openly found support from the basic immorality of human beings, from their organic hope for liberty of morals. It was an unprecedented triumph.

'The film brought in billions of old francs. Just as the creature had escaped from her creator, the success of the film surpassed its promoters. Raoul Levy still shudders when he recalls the day he had been on the point of selling the film rights for a mere $200,000. On the other hand, from this moment onwards Brigitte Bardot refused to write her signature at the foot of a contract for less than thirty million old

This sequence from
Love Is My Profession was
deleted by censors in
several countries

One of the censored scenes from *And God Created Woman*, which Roger Vadim fought so hard to retain

francs. A change indeed from the naive little model who received one hundred francs for posing to be photographed.'

The sensational success of the film not only made Brigitte a star, but made the world aware of French films. Where, previously, they had been confined to Art Theatres and Cinema Clubs, now, with *And God Created Woman* at the forefront, a whole host of pictures from the studios in Paris, Boulogne and Nice flooded the globe. This was an aspect of his triumph which particularly delighted Vadim, for as he said later: 'For the first time the Americans had been shown the female nude on the screen as a work of art, and they had been told that love for the pleasure of loving is not synonymous with sin. The Americans opened their eyes – and the market opened up for French films.

'Hollywood, which was sometimes licentious, but always puritanical, didn't change overnight, but something irreversible had happened. Eight million Americans went to see my film and, although it was often mutilated by women's leagues and local censors, the Americans I meet today still remember it.'

It comes as no surprise to find that after this explosion of worldwide enthusiasm, French critics and audiences found themselves compelled to take another look at the Vadim-Levy-Bardot creation. Nor is it surprising that their initial indifference should have been swept away by the tide of approval from everywhere else. Journalists and critics who had previously ignored, or been less than generous, towards Brigitte, now clamoured for her attention. Her face and her words – real or imagined – were impressed on acres of paper and a survey showed that she had overnight become the subject of forty-seven per cent of French conversations: politics, so long a favourite of French men and women, had been displaced to forty-one per cent.

Little of the real Bardot came out in much of this fevered prose, and in any event she was beginning to build up a healthy dislike for the French press as they relentlessly pursued her – not for information about her work, but on her now evident separation from Vadim and intimate association with Jean-Louis Trintignant. Yet she did talk with some candour to a small circulation film journal which has since been seen as a major influence on the French cinema at this time. It was called *Cahiers du Cinema*, and of it the influential critic Penelope Houston wrote in her study, *The Contemporary Cinema* (1963), 'The influence of *Cahiers du Cinema* extended far beyond its comparatively modest circulation. It set the world of film criticism by the ears, recruiting disciples, compelling opponents to think again about their terms of reference . . . The magazine was staffed by potential directors, journalists by default. Given their chance, they erupted into action.'

It was to this magazine that Brigitte gave her opinions in May 1957 as her star began to burn brightly around the world. Even a quarter of a century later this rare and previously untranslated item makes fascinating reading and gives a unique look into BB's mind at this crucial moment in her life. Interviewer Claude de Givray first states his subject's impact on the world:

'Each generation strives for its sensual emancipation,' he wrote, 'and through the body of its screen vamps acknowledges a certain way of life, a certain style of existence. The daring of a woman who smokes, for instance, is incompatible with cinemascope. Is it therefore bold, or simply naive, to wave the name of Brigitte Bardot as a standard-bearer? Yet, like the Bavarian students who claimed the personality of Lola Montes for their palace revolution, I believe that BB is a good thing for the French cinema – and for two reasons: one, she is twenty-two and successful. She encourages producers to believe in youth. Thanks to her, two young producers have made their first films, Michael Boisrond and Roger Vadim. Two, like many American actresses – but very few French ones – BB is an actress of mannerisms. She does not prepare a role, but recites it ready-made. And by so doing she forces the scenario-writers to review their craft and at the same time to realise her real character. BB, as a product of our times, allowed our times to invade the screen!'

De Givray's question and answer session with Brigitte took a suitably novel form in keeping with the style of *Cahiers du Cinema* – an A–Z of her opinions or 'Du Petit ABB Cédaire.' (A Little Alpha BBet):

A for Actresses: Which actresses do you seem to be most like?

BB: Sophia Loren and Marilyn Monroe are the ones I most admire. Marilyn Monroe is fantastic, she started from nothing, and thanks to her own efforts reached the top. On the other hand, I must admit that actresses like Bette Davis leave me quite cold.

B for Brigitte, of course! What do you think of BB?

BB: People tend to think of me as an object, a little animal, but I can prove my independence. My private life has shown that. In any case, I shall always be ready to sacrifice my career to my private life.

C for Cinema: Do you often go to the cinema?

BB: Very rarely, alas. There are many films I should like to see. When they

76

come round, I say to myself: I will go to see them. Then I can't find the time. I am not very fond of those family stories which spread over several generations. James Dean is a marvellous actor, I liked him enormously in *East of Eden*, but in *Giant* he seemed to me less convincing.

D for *Dieu Créa la Femme*

BB: *And God Created Woman* is my best film. Never have I been so much at ease. Vadim knows me so well. All the lines were so natural. Shooting this film was a marvellous experience.

E for Eroticism: I understand that the equivalent of a quarter of an hour was cut from the final version of *And God Created Woman*?

BB: I didn't time it, but there were certainly a lot of cuts, which is a pity. It spoils the rhythm. For example, there was a long scene on a beach when Christian Marquand slipped my dress off as he caressed me. Almost all of that was cut, and I regret it. It was not offensive, because it was beautiful.

F for Femmes Fatales: You are very fond of Marilyn Monroe, but have you seen any of the films of Garbo and Marlene Dietrich – they were very beautiful.

BB: Alas no, I haven't seen them. But I have seen photos of Greta Garbo and Marlene Dietrich – they certainly were beautiful.

G for Gamine: The public loves to see you as 'That saucy little devil', cheeky and mischievous. It seems to me that that does not really correspond to your real character.

BB: Yes, I think I am less mischievous than my pictures suggest.

H for Hollywood?

BB: I love American films. As for going there to film, we shall have to see about that later.

I for Italy: You have made several films in Italy?

BB: Oh yes, it was so funny, it was so much more disorganised than here. You could arrive at the studio at any time and film late into the night. In England, where I made *Doctor at Sea*, it was the opposite. They are very correct and punctual. If you arrive a bit late, they have a very haughty way of making you realise it.

J for Journalism: After making much of your early films, the press seems to be a bit cool towards you at present.

BB: Yes, I am sorry about that. I am no longer the little Brigitte of the early days, who would spend whole days chatting to journalists. I have a lot to do.

M for Modernism.

BB: I like everything that is modern – costume films bore me . . . My character in *And God Created Woman* appealed to me because it corresponds to our times. In contrast I found the one in *The Bride is too Beautiful* much too sugary.

P for Parisienne.

BB: I am enjoying making a film called *Une Parisienne* right now. It makes a change from the 'little animal' I am always portraying. In this I wear evening dresses and play a married woman. It's rather amusing!

Q for Quality: In a future project *En Cas de Malheur* I believe you will be appearing for the first time in a super-production, with people like Georges Simenon and Jean Gabin involved.

BB: Yes, I am very pleased. It is a marvellous part. But I don't believe that the quality of a film just depends on the people involved. There are good little films, just as there are bad costly ones.

R for Roles: Which is your favourite type of role?

BB: The wild characters. I have not seen Jennifer Jones in *The Vixen*, but she must have been very good.

S for Socrates: Not the philosopher, of course, but the little rabbit you carried in your arms in *And God Created Woman*.

BB: Oh, he was sweet. The whole film remains a marvellous memory.

V for Vadim.

BB: Vadim is my favourite director; I have signed a contract for two more films with him. I think they will be wonderful.

Z for Zut: Your dresser is signalling to us, BB, it is time to dress for your next scene.

A for Au Revoir: But BB does not say *Au revoir*. She does not like saying *Au revoir*.

But to return to the year 1957. Even before the clamour had developed over *And God Created Woman*. Brigitte had been back in the Billancourt Studios in March filming *Une Parisienne* for director Michael Boisrond. Another light-hearted comedy, it had Brigitte playing the married daughter of a French Premier who attempts to curb her husband's wandering eye by flirting with a visiting dignitary, Prince Charles – played by the legendary screen Romeo, Charles Boyer. Boyer, then fifty-eight, was impressed with his co-star and enthused to the press, 'She is, say, lively, and impulsive:

a quick study. She does not run around nude. She undresses with great amiability when the script calls for it . . . A very *sympathique* young woman. Most easy to act with. Her secret is to act always like a girl of eighteen, but to do so naturally without the least archness. In my opinion she will become a very good actress.'

No sooner was this romp over, than it was back to more serious business with Roger Vadim and Raoul Levy. In June the trio headed for Torremolinos in Spain to shoot *Les Bijoutiers du Clair de Lune* (*Heaven Fell That Night*) based on a novel by Albert Vidalie and linking BB with a fast-rising young British actor named Stephen Boyd. Although, of course, *And God Created Woman* was only just beginning to make an impact on audiences, Vadim and Levy were evidently bent on surpassing the eroticism of that film in this new project. A convent girl, played by Brigitte, has run off with a man (Boyd) who has murdered her uncle and seduced her aunt, and she then proceeds to spend days having sado-masochistic sex with him holed up in the Spanish mountains.

The picture was beset with problems from the start. The normally reliable Spanish weather turned appalling, Brigitte, undoubtedly tired after her hectic burst of filming, suffered bouts of illness, and Stephen Boyd, though charmed by her beauty, was perplexed by her manners and impulsive style. With difficulty, Vadim managed to shoot the picture, the wild beauty of Spain and Brigitte complementing each other superbly. However, even before work was finished she was declaring to the world's press: 'I want a holiday. I signed too many contracts. I've had to do one film after another. Never any rest between. That's why I'm ill so often. I want to lie in the sun and do nothing and be quiet.' It was her first sign of real temperament.

So on her return to France, Brigitte took a sustained break from filming, fleeing to the South of France and buying the secluded house near St. Tropez which has been her main home ever since. It seemed appropriate in the eyes of the world's now ever-inquisitive press that she should settle by the beach which had made her famous. Soon she was the constant prey of photographers as well as the focal point of tourists who came (hoping) to ogle her, and celebrity seekers who wanted to settle in the area. The house, named *La Madrague* and tucked away in the Bay des Canoubiers, was hidden by high walls, but this did not prevent rapacious pressmen and determined voyeurs from devising all manner of schemes to intrude on her privacy. They all suspected she lived as freely at home as she did on the screen – and there was every reason to believe they were right. As Willi Frischauer has written:

'The tourists poured into St. Tropez in her wake, and, though they could see nothing, revelled in the thought (well founded) that La Bardot was gambolling behind the wall in the nude. Entertaining frequently – men and women – she tended to leave her guests to themselves much of the time. She basked in the sun, swam in the sea which was soon infested with hordes of photographers. The camera which she seduced more effectively than any living performer was forever poised to rape her privacy.'

It was November before Brigitte re-emerged in public, travelling up from the South of France to the Joinville Studios where she was to make a new picture with one of the legendary stars of the French

cinema, Jean Gabin. *En Cas de Malheur* (*Love Is My Profession*) starred her as a prostitute who is defended by a top Paris lawyer (Gabin) against a charge of robbery – and pays his fee with her body. A curious love affair develops between the couple, only to end in tragedy. The film was based on one of George Simenon's powerful crime novels, and the director was another star of the French industry, Claude Autant-Lara. By all accounts, Jean Gabin at first expressed strong reservations about playing opposite Brigitte – 'That thing that goes about naked?' he is said to have told Raoul Levy when discussing the part – but after working with her, declared, 'She's a real pro – a girl who needs affection.'

During the course of the making of this film the subject of Brigitte's need for affection attracted the notice of a good many journalists, Herbert Kretzmer, the *Daily Sketch*'s roving show business reporter, getting something of a scoop when he reported that the cause of the star's problems was a fear that she was ugly! Writing on 19 November from Paris he said: 'Brigitte Bardot, the long-stemmed Gallic gal whose erotic screen personality can be reckoned among the most potent exports of post-war France, is strangely convinced that the world is all wrong about her. A vast, eager public believes she is lovely and eminently desirable. Brigitte herself? She spends lonely, unhappy hours at her bedroom mirror in her seventh-floor Paris apartment . . . persuading herself against all reason and evidence, that she is UGLY. Downright ugly. This is no joke. No publicity gimmick.

'I was told this astonishing story in Paris this week by Charles Bitsch, a young assistant editor of the film journal *Cahiers du Cinema*. "Brigitte is convinced that she is

ugly," Monsieur Bitsch told me. "She is surprised that there can be any man in the world who can find her features attractive. A recent outbreak of facial eczema seriously aggravated this complex. Brigitte regards her body as a compensation for her face. She feels if she shows her body freely, which she does on and off the screen, then her face will not be noticed. Her body is her secret weapon."'

There is no doubt that Brigitte was in low spirits at the end of 1957. It was a classic case of an actress becoming world-famous overnight – and for someone of her temperament and evident insecurity, it placed incredible pressures upon her.

The year also closed with her divorce from Roger Vadim. Though the marriage had long since ceased to have meaning for either of them, the parting was one which probably hit Brigitte harder than she has ever admitted in public – *or* the media has ever given her credit for. The world's press was much more interested in who her latest boyfriend might be, than in giving any thought to what secret traumas might beset her on parting from the man who had changed her life in just a few short years.

The divorce was effected quickly on 6 December in Paris on the grounds of 'incompatibility', the judge declaring that they were equally to blame for the marriage failing, and that they were both guilty of 'seriously insulting' each other. Strangely, with their separation, a new friendship blossomed, and they have since been able to pay tribute to the importance each had in the foundation of the other's career.

Brigitte summed up her feelings at the time quite simply: 'I got a divorce from Vadim because I wanted to be free. I never want to get married again. Vadim is still my best friend. In fact I like him better now than when he was my husband.' And Vadim responded equally generously, 'It was my fault. She had such a disarming childlike face that I could never consider her a woman. I should have slapped her when she looked at another fellow too often. But how could I slap Brigitte? She always had such an innocent look.'

What both knew beyond any doubt was that without the other, the names of Bardot and Vadim would never have blazed their meteoric paths across the cinema screens of the world.

Brooding sensuality and violence were at the heart of *Heaven Fell That Night*, which Brigitte made in Spain in the summer of 1957 with Stephen Boyd and Maruchi Fresno, under the direction of Roger Vadim

1958
The Cult of Bardolatrie

THE BEGINNING OF 1958 saw BB firmly established as the 'Dream Woman' of most of the world's male population. Conversely, though, her personal relationships were not going at all well. Jean-Louis Trintignant, for whom she had left Roger Vadim, had been called-up by the French Army and was also finding that her fame intruded on their romance. He declared, 'I love everything about her except that she is Brigitte Bardot. When I met her she was insufferable. She fancied herself as a big star and it was detestable. But I discovered she was sensitive beneath it all. I said to myself, "This girl is lost and maybe I can bring something to her."' Unfortunately their enforced separation while Jean-Louis was doing his national service did not help their relationship, and although they met whenever he was on leave, reports of outings with other men inflamed him. He promptly walked out of her life.

Another man was waiting just around the corner to move into her affections, however – a dark-haired, very handsome young guitar player named Sacha Distel – but before this new romance really got off the ground, Brigitte became wrapped up in what was to prove her only film of the year, *La Femme et la Pantin* – (*The Girl and the Puppet*), which English and American dis-

tributors were to re-title much more suggestively *A Woman Like Satan*.

Again set in the beautiful background of Spain, the picture required location work in Seville where Brigitte played an impoverished but fiercely independent young girl who resists the advances of a rich bull-breeder (Spanish star Antonio Vilar), obsessed with making her his mistress. She defies all his efforts to buy her, supporting herself instead as a dancer in third-rate nightclubs and even giving private nude shows. When, finally, his rage at her indifference drives him to wreck a nightclub, she succumbs to his wishes.

Once location work was complete, Brigitte and the film crew returned to France to shoot the interior scenes at studios in Boulogne. Here, for the first time in her career, Brigitte refused to give interviews to the assembled journalists from all over the world – America in particular – who were now anxious to catch her every word for the interest of the millions who had been captivated by *And God Created Woman*. There was one exception: an English journalist, Kenneth Passingham, not only gained access to BB but was allowed to watch her at work on the set of the new film. His report, which appeared in the *Sunday Dispatch* of 15 June, is both revealing about her attitudes at the time and a fascinating insight into how a BB film is made. This is what he wrote:

'Twenty-five people are grouped round a four-poster bed containing Brigitte Bardot and Spanish actor Antonio Vilar. And five of them are telling her how to make love.

'All of them, of course, are French. There are the director, Julien Duvivier, the producer, the cameraman, the assistant director, and – underneath the bed – a pop-eyed prop man lies prone and outstretched, waiting to catch a bedside lamp as Miss Bardot knocks it down in an excess of passion.

'This is too much for Miss Bardot, who has been named "The Sex Kitten" and is striving to merit the title. "Let me," she says, "make love in my own way. I know how to love."

'"Do not be silly, Brigitte," says the director, "this is for CinemaScope. It has got to be big. I will show you."

'He shows her. I feel quite exhausted.

'Tape measures are run from the cameras to the girl with the built-in pout and the home-spun hairstyle that is pure Toulouse Lautrec. The pink towelling bathrobe she is wearing over very little else is ruthlessly pulled from her shoulders to denote the scale of passion in this scene.

'Antonio Vilar, her Spanish co-star in this picture, *La Femme et la Pantin*, is moved into position. He wears a black satin dressing-gown, patent leather slippers, a pencil-slim moustache, and a pained expression. I am not surprised. He has been making love for at least two hours, and still he has to achieve authenticity.

'Under the camera's eye he rolls over, grabs a tuft of Bardot's hair and kisses her with all the passion he has left after a lunch at the studio snack-bar.

'Bardot laughs in his tired, handsome face. Then she calls for her dresser and a mirror. She pats her dishevelled hair. Antonio is most annoyed, because this is not in the script. He manipulates his sleek black curls, twists suddenly, and his eyes register strangulated emotion.

'"Kiss Brigitte, Antonio" coaxes the director (this will be the thirtieth time). Antonio groans.

'"I cannot," he whimpers. His eyes are sunken pools of frustration. "I think I 'ave slipped a disc."'

'He rolls off the four-poster and goes off for massage. Brigitte grins wickedly and joins me. "Love," she says "is a very tiring business. And today I have worked very hard. My jaw feels very sore."

'This is the jaw which was dislocated a few days ago when she had to suffer a slap in the face for her cinematic art.

'I looked at this twenty-three-year-old who has suddenly become the No. 1 box office star with a temperament to match. Outside the studio three American columnists were champing at the bit because she had decided not to talk to them. And at the Ritz in Paris certain film people were trying to damp down the wrath of a Miss Hedda Hopper who, it seems, holds a trembling Hollywood in her hand.

'No one, apparently, refuses to see Miss Hopper, an ex-actress who wears silly hats and writes scintillating tit-bits for forty million Americans. Except, of course, Miss Bardot. "Who," she asked simply, "is Hedda Hopper?"

'"She's crazy," said one of the Americans. "They are queueing five blocks in the States to see her picture *And God Created Woman* and the dame says she won't see anybody. I've been here a fortnight."

'The odd thing was he was prepared to stay another fortnight for a word with Bardot.

84

'In her dressing-room, where she has a record-player and a stack of swing discs, including a couple of Sinatra offerings, Miss Bardot relaxed, twiddled her bare feet.

'"I was hoping to see Sinatra," she said. "I thought he was coming to Paris to see me and discuss the picture we are going to do together in November. He is a naughty boy."

'With the knowledge that Mr Sinatra had skipped Paris for Rome and a word in the ear of Ava Gardner, I agreed with Miss Bardot.

'"I like naughty boys," said Miss Bardot, slipping the bathrobe from her shoulders. "But at the moment my career comes first. I have no time for the private life."

'The private life, I can reveal, is lived in a two-floor apartment in the Trocadero district of Paris with a maid, a secretary, a pigeon, a couple of canaries, and a stray dog she plucked from the streets of Madrid. Gone is ex-husband producer Vadim. "These days I always sleep well," said Miss Bardot, "and always, I regret to say it, in the nude."

'Her big bold eyes did not flicker. "I am not anxious at the moment to acquire another husband. I like my freedom too much. But if the right man came along I would marry him tomorrow. I like men. The most important thing in the world is love. What attracts me most in a man? I will tell you the points I look for. First – his mouth, then his teeth, and then his sincerity."

'Idly I wondered how Mr Sinatra would make out when they meet. For this primitive produce of Paris needs no psychiatrist. Already she has assessed herself and her potential.

'"There is, at the moment," she said, "a cult which I will call Bardolatrie. Now, suddenly, everyone worships me. American producers are queueing on their knees to get me on the screen. But I know the cult will pass – all too soon. In three years it will all be over.

'"I shall leave the screen at twenty-five – when my beauty begins to fade. I shall not be too sorry. There will be other reasons for living."

'I asked for the reasons and the Bardot pout parted to reveal even white teeth.

'"L'Amour," she said, "do you not think it is the biggest thing in the world?"

'She slipped off her robe, put a disc on the record player. Its title? *This is Sinatra*.

'Down the corridor Antonio was groaning. His disc had really slipped.'

The project which Brigitte mentioned for a film co-starring Frank Sinatra, then the world's leading popular singer, was something that had been occupying Raoul Levy since the end of the previous year – but like Brigitte's personal relationships then, it too was doomed to failure.

Levy had dreamed up the idea of bringing about a screen match of 'The Voice' and 'The Broad of Broads' (as Sinatra might have called Brigitte). He believed it would be 'the greatest chemical fusion since nitroglycerine' and had found what he considered to be the ideal vehicle for them – a musical comedy *Paris by Night* in which Sinatra would play a failed impressario drinking himself to death who is saved from his fate by a beautiful dancing girl.

To begin with all the signs were good. Levy, along with Roger Vadim, flew to California to see Sinatra and secured his interest in the project. A screenplay was worked on by Vadim and an American,

Harry Kurnitz, and Brigitte even began to talk of the plot in interviews during the autumn. 'It will not be sexy like my other films,' she said. 'I sleep in the bath. He kills himself in my car.'

By November 1957 *Paris by Night* seemed on the verge of going before the cameras. The world – and the world's press – waited with baited breath to see how the two stars would react to each other. Then disaster struck. Sinatra refused point blank to film in Paris. Bardot must come to Hollywood, he said. Brigitte, who was terrified of flying, insisted the picture be shot in Paris – where it was set, after all. Impasse. Two superstars unwilling to bend. And that was the end of arguably the most intriguing film

Brigitte Bardot – and Frank Sinatra, for that matter – might ever have made.

If Brigitte was in any way upset with the failure of this project, she soon pushed it to one side – in the arms of the guitarist, Sacha Distel, whom she met as she was completing work on *La Femme et le Pantin*. Their love affair was to be a round of dreamy, magical days and nights at *La Madrague* and St. Tropez, as summer sped through autumn, winter and into the following year. But, ultimately it, too, was doomed. Recently, Sacha, now a showbusiness legend himself, and still almost as darkly handsome as he

Brigitte with Sacha Distel, her new love in 1958

Controversy over a pair of spectacles! Brigitte claims not to have authorised this use of her likeness in advertising, although a signed contract is produced when she threatens to sue

was when he first met BB, talked about their eight-month romance for the first time.

'I met Brigitte when I was twenty-five', he said. 'I had just started to sing about a year before and although I was a well-known jazz guitarist, I had not made a hit record. For Brigitte it was quite different. When we met she was at her peak. Everything had happened to her. And that's what ruined things between us. I might have been well known and independent, but I wasn't as well known as she was. And this counted against me. It got me a bad reputation. During our romance, I was regarded by the outside world as Brigitte Bardot's latest plaything. In the beginning it was the perfect summer romance. Then the press made it sound different, and our situation started to become difficult.

'The most important thing about any woman I was going to marry is that she would be the mother of my children. It took Brigitte and me a few months to find out that she was not going to be the mother of my children. And I wasn't going to be the father of her child. Brigitte was somebody who needed the man she was in love with to be with her constantly. To do the things she wanted to do. To take second place. And that was not what I had in mind at all. You see, I was working very hard at the time to become Sacha Distel, successful singer – not Mr Bardot. If Brigitte had felt like it, she could have been Mrs Distel. There was never any doubt in my mind that any woman I married would be Mrs Distel.'

Strangely, in the light of what Sacha Distel says about Brigitte's concern for her identity at this time, in the following year two of her most firmly held beliefs were to go by the board. First, she was to star in a film in which she turned her back completely on her 'sex symbol' image. Secondly, and perhaps most surprisingly, she was to get married again and have a baby.

Brigitte looking anything but *A Woman Like Satan* in a shot from her 1958 film

90

1959
Lady Godiva with Clothes

OR THE LAST of his four contracted films with Brigitte Bardot, Raoul Levy had something very different in mind, as he announced to the press on New Year's Day, 1959, 'You can't hit the jackpot twice. I have now made my last sex film.' (Although both *Heaven Fell That Night* and *A Woman Like Satan* were complete, neither had been released at that moment.) 'As far as I am concerned you will never again see Brigitte nude or nearly nude or jumping in and out of bed in any film of mine. That is over. You can have too much of a good thing. She is going to England to make a film called *Babette S'En Va-t-En Guerre* (released as *Babette Goes to War*) in which she becomes a member of the British Secret Service and you will see her being trained by a typical British sergeant-major to parachute into France. Naturally, as she's in the British Secret Service she has to keep her clothes on. It's sort of traditional, isn't it? And there are certain things you simply don't do in a parachute.'

Levy also told the press that he hoped Brigitte's co-star would be David Niven.

When this plan fell through, however, he went after the Italian heart-throb Rossano Brazzi, but again was unable to secure the star's services. The word around the film business was that most leading men were worried about being overshadowed by Brigitte – 'When she's on the screen who's going to look at anyone else?' one star commented wryly. Raoul Levy, getting more than a little worried, even proposed that Brigitte's current love, Sacha Distel, might play opposite her. But when this idea, too, came to nothing, BB came up with her own suggestion. On a recent visit to the cinema in Paris, she had seen a film called *Les Tricheurs* and been visibly impressed by the leading man, tall, dark-haired Jacques Charrier. When she went to see him again on the stage in *The Diary of Anne Frank* she was sure he was the right man for the part. And from the start there were all the signs he was also right to play a rather more intimate role in her life.

To film her part as a bordello maid who is evacuated at Dunkirk in 1940 and then parachuted back into France as a spy to help foil the German invasion plans, Brigitte flew to London later that month. Once again her beauty captivated everyone at Pinewood Studios along with over 200 Airmen at RAF Station Abingdon in Berkshire who gave up their leave to help shoot a number of location scenes.

Some of the strain of filming *The Truth* shows in this candid off-the-set photograph taken in September 1960

During her work both in England and back in France at the St. Maurice Studios in Paris, Brigitte remained remote from the press, issuing a simple statement about why she had chosen a completely new type of role. 'I am sick of sex,' she said. 'And what they have made me out to be. I do not like it any more – and I think maybe other people are sick of it, too. This is my first sexless film. I want everyone under sixteen to be able to see me.' On the surface, this seemed a typical exercise in generating public interest in a picture that was quite different from those BB had done before. But there has always been more to Brigitte than at first seems apparent in her public statements, and when one British journalist, John Crueseman, did manage to get her to speak more fully about her feelings, something much more revealing emerged. She was quite genuinely getting tired of the treadmill of films onto which she had been thrust. This is what she told Crueseman:

'I am not really interested in the cinema. When I started in films six years ago I loathed it, and to speak truly I don't enjoy it even now as I suppose one ought to enjoy one's work. I live from day to day. If the fame that has been my lucky chance were to stop tomorrow, I would not mind. No doubt many who read this will say: "Ah, but that is what she pretends – just wait and see." But, you know, I do not greatly care what people say now, for I have learned that life would become a torture if I did worry. So I just say "Zut" to everyone.

'When you find yourself in this strange position of semi-goddess, which is so unnatural anyway, publicity takes its revenge on you. People are forever finding something wrong with you. If you hit back, you are being difficult. If you give the wrong answers – and it is not always easy to give the right ones – the words sound dreadful.

'The film world is an absurd world. Against it I react not so as to be different, but because I am quite determined to live my own life as I am made, not as others make me. When I work I am all right. When I think about it all I am horrified at the extraordinary image that has been created about me. I am not superficial, and I am not ungrateful. I know very well what goes on. I want to keep a balance without letting life become distorted. That is not easy. For the life of Brigitte Bardot, film star, and the life of Brigitte Bardot, Parisienne like a million others – they are incompatible. But I have to live with both myselves as best I may.

'Naturally I enjoy the advantages stardom brings. I make a lot of money. And I do not despise money. Why should I? What is more I make a lot of money, too, for others who need it. That is good. I am able to live as I want to. I can buy more than most women. I like to wear what pleases me, not what people think I ought to wear. This has its penalties too. If I wear something simple, even casual, people say I am negligent. I don't care, I ought to know better. If I wear grand clothes, then I am supposed to be putting on airs and making myself ridiculous by playing the great lady. It is just not worthwhile dressing for the role of film star. Sometimes I have beautiful dresses made at one of the great couturiers. Often I just buy a frock off the peg. Fortunately my measurements are good. No one dictates fashion to me, and I do not imagine I should dictate fashion to them. When I attended the great Callas Gala at the Paris Opera a short time ago, where everyone was dressed to kill, I wore something quite simple; no jewellery, just a rose in my hair.

I aimed to appear at my best in the way that suited me. I did not do it to look bizarre. That way you only end by appearing to be silly.'

Crueseman asked Brigitte how she was coping with the still-growing cult of Bardo-latrie.

'I refuse to be submerged in a cult,' she said. 'I insist on remaining myself. It is hard enough in this film fantasy world to be sure of oneself. I am a star despite myself. It is odd looking back to the time ten years ago when I was a young girl. I cannot remem-ber being interested in film stars. I was not stage struck although I loved the ballet. There was no Bardot for me whom I wanted to try to look like. It never occurred to me that I was out of the ordinary. In fact, I do not think I am. For a while when I began filming I honestly thought I was ugly. I could not believe otherwise. Evidentally I am not. I have just fitted the

On location in England making *Babette Goes To War*, Brigitte was very popular with paratroopers at Abingdon – even though she was in full battle dress!

mood of the times. What tomorrow's mood will bring tomorrow will show. It is no use breaking one's heart wondering about that.

'I have no pretensions to becoming a great actress. There is no part I long to play. I know I shall never be asked to appear at the *Comédie Française*. That does not worry me for I do not wish to be an actress at all costs. I hope to play different roles in the sort of films I can act in. If the script says I should undress, then I undress. It does not matter greatly one way or the other. All I want to do, all I can ever hope to do, is to perfect myself playing myself.'

Brigitte's evident coming to terms with herself and her fame was also carried into *Babette Goes To War* which later earned praise from many of the critics. Even those who had derided her previously as nothing more than a sex object, praised her skill as a comedienne. Paul Dehn, the highly-regarded critic of the now-defunct *News Chronicle*, spoke for many when he wrote, 'Here, all of a sudden, is Bardot the polished comedienne; and the week's nicest surprise is to see her squaring her incomparable shoulders in readiness to receive the mantle which Danielle Darrieux must one day, alas, pass on . . . I laughed fit to bust. Best comedy of the year.'

Other changes had occurred in Brigitte's life during the making of this film. Her love affair with Sacha Distel had cooled and in April she issued a brief statement through her secretary: 'Mlle Bardot asks me to announce that she has severed all relations with M. Sacha Distel.' It came as no surprise to anyone who had watched Brigitte working on the set with her co-star Jacques Charrier, to learn that he was the new man in her life. But what did surprise them was when, two months after this announce-ment, Brigitte and Jacques got married.

Charrier, who came from a distinguished French military family, was, however, sub-jected to considerable pressures from his father, Colonel Charrier, who categorically opposed the marriage. His misgivings were shown to be well founded when the wed-ding ceremony took place in absolute shambles. It was surely an omen of what was to come. The couple had naturally tried to keep their plans secret: but when they arrived on the morning of 18 June at Louveciennes Town Hall, near Paris, the little village that had been a weekend retreat for the Bardot family since Brigitte was a child, they found the place besieged by journalists and photographers. As one report had it, 'While police reinforcements were being brought up to keep the photo-graphers at bay, the bride and bridegroom were ushered into the mayor's office. The shutters were closed, the doors locked. There was nearly a riot when Charrier and the couple's fathers fought photographers who broke down the town hall door.' As soon as the ceremony was over, the couple fled to what they hoped would be a peaceful and private honeymoon at *La Madrague*. But, as Donald Zec of the *Daily Mirror* reported, 'Not since Lady Godiva stripped to canter through Coventry has one girl thrown a town into such a tizzy.'

Surprised though the world had been by this sudden marriage of the world's most famous sex symbol – it was even more sur-prised when Madame Charrier announced that she was pregnant. Her feelings were obviously ambivalent as this press quote made clear: 'I never do anything by chance,' she said. 'But I don't find preg-nancy much of a joy. I'm certainly fright-ened of childbirth. But I'm afraid I can't find a way of avoiding it.'

Her condition did not prevent Brigitte continuing to work, however, for on 15 July she clocked in at the Studios La Victorine in Nice to begin work on *Voulex-vous Danser Avec Moi?* (released abroad as *Come Dance With Me*). The picture reunited her with director Michel Boisrond who announced, 'Our first two films were pure comedy. This time I wanted a change – a suspense film with some comedy touches. Because for me, Brigitte is one of the rare actresses who can combine humour and drama.'

Brigitte played the wife of a dentist who had been wrongly accused of the murder of a sexy dance school instructress. She joins the company to unmask the real villain and in a surprise denouement reveals the killer to be a transvestite. Although work on the film went along smoothly enough as Brigitte advanced in her pregnancy (which was not noticeable on the screen), two tragedies did undermine the generally

A dramatic moment in the hands of Gestapo chief, Francis Blanche, in *Babette Goes To War*

happy atmosphere. Sylvia Lopez, the girl first picked to play the blackmailer fell ill after a few days' shooting and died of leukaemia (she was replaced by Dawn Adams), while co-star Henri Vidal lived only a few days after work was completed.

Off-screen, ill-health also reared its ugly head in Brigitte's own life. In the autumn, husband Jacques was called up for military service, and no sooner had he joined his regiment than he fell ill. With Brigitte for a wife, and a colonel for a father (not to mention three brothers on active service in Algeria), Jacques became the centre of a press furore with all manner of suggestions being made concerning his illness – ranging from jealousy to malingering. The matter even reached the French Assembly, which prompted that most sedate and reliable of British newspapers, *The Times*, to attempt to put the matter in perspective amidst all the hysteria and speculation. The paper carried this report from its Paris correspondent on 20 November:

'Two questions were asked yesterday, one in the National Assembly and the other in the Paris municipal council, about special leave granted to M. Jacques Charrier, the husband of the French film actress Brigitte Bardot, who recently joined the colours for his military service. M. Charrier, who played the part of an army officer in Mlle Bardot's latest film, *Babette Goes To War*, was given forty-eight hours' leave by his regiment, which is stationed at Orange, and, according to press reports, this was a concession granted after a telegram had been received from his wife (who is expecting a child) saying that she was unwell. M. Charrier, who had already been in the Orange military hospital with eye trouble, is reported to have been taken ill while on leave in Paris, and is now in hospital.

'In the Assembly a neo-Gaullist Deputy asked the Government what measures it proposed to take to ensure that all recruits were treated in the same way, "even when they come from a big fashion house or from the arms of a great actress". Recent press reports, he said, had contained "shocking accounts" for anyone who had a son with the colours. The Press reports mentioned alleged that M. Charrier was seen out and about with his wife during his forty-eight hours' leave, and that he was also occupied in putting the finishing touches to his latest film.'

Whatever the truth was about this extraordinary sequence of events in November 1959, the outcome was that Jacques Charrier was discharged from the Army just three months after his call-up as *inapte à servir*. It was to leave a scar on Charrier himself as well as on his marriage.

However the mixed fortunes in her private life may have affected Brigitte during 1959, she did not need to worry for one moment about her status as an international star, for newspapers all over the world greeted her twenty-fifth birthday in September with extensive profiles. Britain's prestigious Sunday paper *The Observer* was a leader among these, writing:

'The French film star Miss Brigitte Bardot, who is twenty-five, shares with Mr Krushchev the distinction of being recognised throughout the world by her initials alone. In Europe, the Americas and the Far East, the letters "BB" produce a marked response even from people who have seen none of Miss Bardot's films. The spread and speed of her rise to fame are a tribute to the power and efficiency of modern means of communication. For her establishment as a "sex symbol" owes at least as much to the international publicity machine as to her cinema appearances.

'The advertising campaign which made her as well known as the master of the Soviet Union did not merely make clever use of long blonde hair, a rare shape and lips set in a childish pout. Nor did it promise brilliant new talent. In Miss Bardot's case, the publicity men persuaded the world that she was "authentic" – the same person both on the screen and off. They sold a personality, not an actress.'

The newspaper went on to claim that the basis of the Bardot myth was 'the combination of childish face and mature body, innocence and sexuality' and continued: 'The Bardot child-woman is never sentimental or mysterious. She has no time for the tantalising wiles of a Cleopatra. She is a frank man-hunter and her methods of seduction are forthright – she lifts her skirt or bites her partner's shoulder to indicate what she has in mind. Colette's Gigi has to be taught about sex, BB, though as young, knows about it and enjoys it for its own sake.'

But perhaps, asked *The Observer*, the child-woman was already on the way out – having reached her ultimate expression in Nabokov's *Lolita* and Raymond Queneau's bestselling novel, *Zazie Dans Le Metro*, about an immensely knowing, foul-mouthed little girl impatient of adult pretence and stupidity?

'Miss Bardot is evidently aware of the need for change,' the newspaper goes on, 'and is no longer content with parts that are "just pretty pictures", but she is too good a business woman to destroy her profitable myth out of hand. Her problem is to establish a new meaning to her initials without losing the international credit that at present goes with them. But to the countless devotees of "Bardolatrie", a mature, adult BB may appear a contradiction in terms.'

For Brigitte, at the end of her first decade in films and on the verge of giving birth to a child, the year ahead was obviously full of hidden fears as well as posing a number of unavoidable questions about her future. In truth, it was destined to be a time of both great joy and the deepest despair.

On 19 June 1959, Brigitte married Jacques Charrier, her co-star in *Babette Goes To War*

99

1960
'La Tragedienne'

THE YEAR 1960 was only a few days old when Bébé presented her husband Jacques Charrier with a lusty baby son. The 7lb 4oz child was born at 2.31 on the morning of 11 January – at the couple's Paris flat, 71 Avenue Paul Doumer. The world, which had been waiting with mounting excitement for the news, greeted Charrier's announcement of the event – which he made in the Café Royale, a few doors down the street from the couple's apartment, with joyous enthusiasm. As Tony Crawley has written:

'The birth was more eagerly anticipated than Neil Armstrong's giant leap for mankind less than ten years later. The French forgot their Algerian war along with their GNP and the national debt, their big little *bombe atomique* and their fears of the resurgent Germany. Even Charrier's contretemps with the army were forgiven in the country's unified happiness as their Bébé – yes, she was theirs now – was about to attain respectability as a mother. A married mother at that.'

While Brigitte's father hurried off to register the infant's name, Nicolas-Jacques Charrier, husband Jacques faced the assembled press declaring that he had 'never been happier in my life'. He said he had held his wife's hand throughout her labour and was 'impressed by the lusty crying voice of my son'. Initially, Jacques was unable to tell the waiting throng of reporters the baby's weight because, according to one story, 'although the flat had all the latest obstetrical equipment, someone had forgotten to provide scales!'

Hardly able to hear himself think over the babble of voices, Jacques tried to reply to questions about who the child resembled. The boy had dimples like his own, he said (though these had almost disappeared during the traumatic weeks of army service) and Brigitte had already nicknamed him, 'Fossettes'. And what of the mother herself? According to Charrier she had asked the doctor after the birth, 'Is it a boy?' And on being told it was, had cried, '*Chic alors!*' And would she breastfeed the infant? No, it was to be bottle-fed.

In the days immediately following her confinement, Brigitte appeared to want to distance herself completely from her old identity. 'The initials BB should take all the criticism,' she said, 'I am another person who lives just how she wants to. I often read descriptions and commentaries that don't correspond with reality. I think they're talking about a stranger.' And, as if to confirm this statement, she allowed British journalist Gerald Fairlie, who later wrote a six-part series on her life and legend, a peep into her domestic life – which he promptly portrayed as being much like that of any normal Parisienne:

'Brigitte Bardot lives with her husband Jacques Charrier in a modest flat in a modest area of Paris, not very far from an unfashionable corner of the Bois de Boulogne,' wrote Fairlie. 'It is just about the last place in which I would expect her to live – comfortable, but in no way luxurious. Before I met her I imagined that she must live in lush luxury in some smart place like one of the expensive flats in the great old private houses which line the avenue from the Arc de Triomphe to the Bois, on the way to Longchamps.

'After the birth of little Nicolas, she and Charrier did not move to a larger flat in a more fashionable area, which some might think would have been a more suitable home for an international star and her actor husband. They merely took a flat adjacent to the one they were already occupying in the same building. This they converted into a nursery and also an office for Charrier. The Bardot flat is furnished plainly but comfortably in what may perhaps be best described as old English inn furniture, but which Charrier describes as rustic. Inside it is as unassuming as the building is outside.

'When Brigitte Bardot is not working, what is her average day? She rises at a reasonable hour, of course, but not with the dawn. And for most of the day she scarcely leaves her home. She loves nothing better than decorating and redecorating, doing everything possible herself. She loves pottering about her home, thinking out and making improvements, dressed certainly most informally, probably – as I first saw her – in a boy's high-necked green sweater, blue jeans and yellow sandals. She will have made up her eyes, because she always does, but otherwise she will be unadorned. No lipstick, no powder, no perfume, just Brigitte Bardot, the ungilded lily.

'She likes the ordinary chores of a housewife. She seldom takes a drink, though she will have one or two when at one of the infrequent parties which she consents to attend. The sort of party she likes is to have a few of her friends call in informally and stay to dinner. The sort of party which develops unexpectedly, and where everyone is a close friend. And most nights, early to bed. That is the real Brigitte Bardot, the reigning symbol of sex.'

However much the 'reigning symbol of sex' might have given the impression to Fairlie that she wanted a life of domestic bliss, three months after the birth of Nicolas-Jacques, she went back to work on a new film. The picture was called *La Vérité* (*The Truth*) and under the direction of one of the masters of the French cinema, Henri-Georges Clouzot, Brigitte set out to show that she could be a fine dramatic actress as well as a sex symbol and a comedienne. The part she played, of Dominique Marceau, was a challenging one – as well as containing certain parallels to her own life.

Dominique is a beautiful, amoral young woman who has rejected her bourgeois upbringing and thrown herself into a series of affairs. One of these is with Gilbert Tellier, an up-and-coming musician, who after a passionate interlude rejects her for the sake of his career. In a dramatic confrontation she threatens to kill herself unless he returns: but in a struggle for the gun she is hiding, Gilbert is shot and killed. Much of the action of the film takes place during the subsequent trial with Brigitte vividly re-enacting the *crime passionnel*. But love is never simple nor uncomplicated, and unable to explain precisely what happened, Dominique denies the jury the chance to pass judgement on her by slashing her wrists in her cell and taking her own life. The closing scene was to have a grim echo later the same year.

Brigitte was enthusiastic about the part – and the man she had personally selected to play the part of Gilbert, Sami Frey. (Indeed, they were soon to be lovers.) Speaking of the picture, she enthused: 'This is my favourite film. Very important to me. It is the first really dramatic picture I have made. I can act in it. There are two parts for me in it. One is like BB – dancing the cha-cha and all that. And there is another part in court where the girl is accused of murdering her lover. In the first part of the film, I'm very gay – like BB – but in the second part, I'm very serious. I end up killing myself in jail. I have had to work harder on this film than I have ever worked before in my life.'

Director Clouzot, with his reputation as a hard task master and his determination to push his actors and actresses to the very peak of their powers, worked Brigitte strenuously whether she was playing a dramatic moment during the trial scenes or writhing in bed with Sami Frey. Not surprisingly, news of this drive for authenticity earned the production the headline: '*Et Clouzot créa la tragédienne!*'

The French film magazine, *Cinemonde*, later investigated the mass of rumours which surrounded the picture and put the matter into clearer perspective in an article entitled, 'A Vulnerable Tormentor'. 'Clouzot the Terrible! Clouzot the Sorcerer! Clouzot the Star-Crusher! This is everyone's idea of the man,' said the magazine, 'especially after all the tales about *La Vérité*. Why, he himself admitted, "I am very demanding with my actors, just as I am demanding of myself. I imagine very clearly the way I am going to film, and I torture people to obtain exactly what I want."

'But what did the gossip writers make of this talk of "torture"? No less than that Brigitte Bardot's love for Charrier could not possibly stand up to the way in which Clouzot threw her into the arms of Sami Frey. Hence the "cruelties" on the film set were said to have completely demoralised BB, leading her gradually to the idea of suicide (regardless of the fact that she publicly denied this). What was Clouzot's answer, for example, referring to tortures inflicted on BB? "If I struck her," he said "it was for the final scene of *La Vérité*. She begged me: 'I have to cry. Help me!' And afterwards she said that we would end our days together!"'

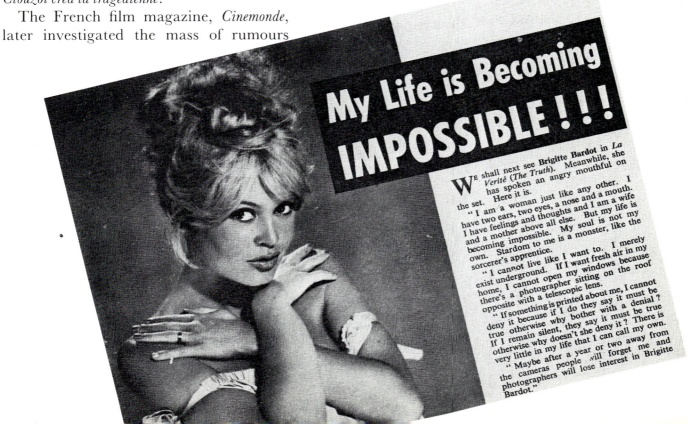

My Life is Becoming IMPOSSIBLE !!!

WE shall next see Brigitte Bardot in *La Vérité* (The Truth). Meanwhile, she has spoken an angry mouthful on the set. Here it is.

"I am a woman just like any other. I have two ears, two eyes, a nose and a mouth. I have feelings and thoughts and I am a wife and a mother above all else. But my life is becoming impossible. My soul is not my own. Stardom to me is a monster, like the sorcerer's apprentice.

"I cannot live like I want to. I merely exist underground. If I want fresh air in my home, I cannot open my windows because there's a photographer sitting on the roof opposite with a telescopic lens.

"If something is printed about me, I cannot deny it because if I do they say it must be true otherwise why bother with a denial? If I remain silent, they say it must be true otherwise why doesn't she deny it? There is very little in my life that I can call my own.

"Maybe after a year or two away from the cameras people will forget me and photographers will lose interest in Brigitte Bardot."

Cinemonde concluded, 'Truth to tell, it seems that of the "harm" done by Clouzot, he himself was the first victim – for his life thereafter became more and more one of tragedy.'*

Regardless of the pain – real or imagined – which it cost to make *The Truth*, it was later to be highly acclaimed by the critics and won the *Grand Prix du Cinema Français*. Clouzot also got the best director award at the 1961 Mar Del Plat festival in Argentina, and Brigitte was named Best Foreign Actress for this performance at the Italian Film Festival in the same year.

As well as the emotional maelstrom of making this film, Brigitte was also embroiled in her own private troubles as the year went on. Jacques Charrier's health got worse and she decided to put baby Nicolas in the care of his relatives. Consequently, hardly a day passed without her name appearing in headlines of one sort or another. She expressed her feelings vividly about this state of affairs while filming was still taking place.

'I cannot resent being big news,' she said, 'except that it compels me to be very lonely, for I can have next to no private life. Professionally, I must welcome it. But there is no excuse for inventing news about me. My complaint is that if there is nothing genuine to say about me perhaps every two days, then the French Press will invent something and the lie may be repeated throughout the world, if it is juicy enough.

'I can give you examples. Only recently, when there was nothing genuine to say

about me for a few days, they printed a story that I had rented a house in Brittany for a holiday. If this is news, it is also news to me. I have never contemplated renting a house in Brittany in my life. I agree that this example is unimportant. But many things have been written, and been published, which are totally untrue and which have given me the most intense pain and might well have ruined my private, even my public, life.

'You know that recently my husband was very ill and had to go into a nursing home. At just about the same time Georges Clouzot's wife also became ill and also had to go into a nursing home. The papers had the audacity to imply that all this had been arranged in order to leave us – Clouzot and me – free to have an affair together. Are you surprised that I am disgusted? This might have killed my happiness. And it no doubt lost me many fans, for who would want to like a girl who could do such a thing?'

They were prophetic words. Because it was becoming evident that much of the French public's love for Brigitte which they had demonstrated at the start of the year when her baby was born, was gradually evaporating. How had this dramatic change of affairs come about? London journalist Joan Harrison, who had covered the early days of Brigitte's rise to fame and seen Roger Vadim's part in it, had the bright idea of asking him. Could he explain the 'resentment and almost hate' which now existed in France against Brigitte 'or rather the person the public believe her to be'?

'The French are the most reactionary people in the world,' Vadim told her. 'The English and the Americans tend to think that life is freer in France because there is more surface liberty. But the French mid-

* Henri-Georges Clouzot (1907–1977) suffered poor vision and ill-health for many years which seriously affected his work both as a screenwriter and director. A number of his projects had to be aborted as a result of his declining condition, and during the last years of his life he spent some time in a sanitorium.

dle-class, while appearing to live a freer life, actually don't. They are more easily shocked and resent any fundamental change. The English seem to be more conformist on the outside but are deliciously mad inside.'

Such, indeed, was the interest generated in this change of attitude towards Brigitte, that it attracted the attention of one of the country's leading philosophers, Simone de Beauvoir, author of the classic study on women, *The Second Sex*. In August 1960 she published a brilliant short study entitled *Brigitte Bardot and the Lolita Syndrome*, which for many unbiased observers cut right to the heart of the matter with the precision of a surgeon's knife. What she said, in a nutshell, was that the French were *afraid* of Brigitte Bardot.

Three months after the birth of Nicolas-Jacques, Brigitte is back in the film studios with director, Henri-Georges Clouzot, filming what is to prove her favourite picture, *The Truth*

Mlle de Beauvoir set out to link Brigitte's popularity with the cult of the 'child-woman' as personified by Lolita, the twelve-year-old heroine of Vladimir Nabokov's novel. Bardot, she said, was the perfect specimen of the 'ambiguous nymph' – seen from behind, her slender, muscular dancer's body was almost androgynous, but there was no denying that 'femininity triumphs in her delightful bosom'.

'Her hair-do is that of a negligent waif,' wrote Mlle de Beauvoir. 'The line of her lips forms a childish pout, and at the same time those lips are very kissable. She goes barefoot, turns up her nose at elegant clothes, jewels, girdles, perfumes, make-up, at all artifice. Yet her walk is lascivious, and a saint would sell his soul to the devil merely to watch her dance.'

To many people this may sound just what a Frenchman would want. But, went on Mlle de Beauvoir, Frenchmen don't have the Lolita complex. What they can't forgive is that her eroticism is *aggressive*. In the game of love she was as much the hunter as the prey.

'She wounded masculine pride. In Latin countries like France, where men clung to the myth of woman as "an object," her naturalness seemed perverse. To spurn jewels, cosmetics, high heels and girdles is to refuse to turn oneself into a remote idol. It is to assert that one is man's equal and that between woman and man there is equal mutual desire and pleasure. The male feels uncomfortable if, instead of a doll of flesh and blood, he holds in his arms a conscious being who is sizing him up.'

In France women were accomplices in this feeling of male superiority, she said. Frenchmen preferred the servility of the doll to the haughty shamelessness of Bardot. 'They don't like her,' said Mlle de Beauvoir, 'because they are unwilling to give up their role of Lord and Master.' But to older Englishmen and Americans, Bardot was a Lolita type. Mlle de Beauvoir went on: 'The adult woman, driving a car, unceremoniously displaying her nudity on beaches, even speculating on the Stock Exchange, inhabits the same world as the man, but the child-woman moves in a universe which he cannot enter. The age difference establishes between them the distance which seems necessary for desire.'

Mlle de Beauvoir also had an idea why Brigitte had become the idol of the young – almost the goddess of the rebel generation. 'Bardot', she wrote, 'does not try to scandalise. She has no demands to make; she is no more conscious of her rights than of her duties. She follows her inclinations. She eats when she is hungry and makes love with the same unceremonious simplicity. Desire and pleasure seem more convincing than precepts and conventions. She does as she pleases, and that is what is most disturbing. She rejects not only hypocrisy and reprimands but prudence, calculation and predetermination of any kind. For her the future is still one of those adult inventions in which she has no confidence.' Whether Brigitte read this analysis of her appeal is not known (it is a fact, though, that she rarely reads *anything* about herself, and has not done so for years), yet Mlle de Beauvoir had undoubtedly perceived something very crucial in her character when she spoke of her lack of confidence in the future. In that autumn of 1960, as she worked on *La Vérité*, Brigitte was riddled with doubts about herself and her future. These doubts manifested themselves in one of the saddest episodes of her life – a second attempt at suicide.

Early in September Brigitte issued a

statement from the set of *La Vérité* which, with hindsight, reveals much of her private agony. It clearly showed how she feared the pressures building up around her. 'I am a woman just like any other,' Brigitte said (with what can only be described as massive understatement.) 'I have two ears, two eyes, a nose and a mouth. I have feelings and thoughts and I am a wife and mother above all else. But my life is becoming impossible. My soul is not my own any more. Stardom to me is a monster; it is like the spell cast by the sorcerer's apprentice. I cannot live as I want to. I merely exist underground. If I want fresh air in my home, I cannot open my window because there's a photographer sitting on the roof with a telescopic lens. I would like to give up films if this continues . . .'

In the week around her twenty-sixth birthday, events reached crisis point. On Saturday, 24 September she declared, 'Whatever I do is held against me. Fame has brought me so much unhappiness. If only every man who sees my films did not get the impression he can make love to me I would be a lot happier.' Two days later she was saying, 'I am tired and worn out. I can't make my mind up about anything.'

Then, with filming at last complete, Brigitte fled from the set of *La Vérité*, and

Brigitte in *The Truth* with co-star, Sami Frey. Soon he was to become her lover

went into hiding at the home of some friends, Jean-Claude Simon and his wife Mercedes, at Carbolles near Menton. Despite the secrecy a posse of journalists managed to find her and on the evening of her birthday she screamed at them: 'Leave me alone! I'm going to die anyway.'

Within hours those words had almost come true. A neighbour of the Simons', thirteen-year-old Jean-Louis Bournos, suddenly heard a strange noise from the darkened garden and, going to investigate, found Brigitte's unconscious body. There were deep cuts on both wrists and a razor blade lay nearby. Frantically, she was rushed to the St. François Hospital in Nice and her life was saved by a hair's breadth. Another twenty minutes, said a doctor, and she would have been dead. Examination also showed that she had swallowed a whole bottle of sleeping pills.

In the Simons' villa a graphic but garbled note in Brigitte's handwriting was found. It underlined that her public statements had been more than just anger, they were truly a *cri de coeur*:

'I am full of the blues,' the note read, 'I am desperate and unhappy. I am changing my ideas. I am in pain and I might as well suffer for something. See you later. B.'

With her family and a few friends at her bedside, Brigitte made a quick recovery. But though the physical scars of her ordeal soon faded, her hate for the pressures of the media which she believed had brought about this breakdown deepened still further. 'They refused to leave,' she said, 'and to me they looked like an ugly black octopus trying to pull me away from my simple life. Something went snap. There seemed no way out. I tried to stop falling away. It was no good. I couldn't stop myself. I spun in darkness, ran out into the garden in panic. The world had come to an end for Brigitte Bardot.'

Thankfully, the world did not come to an end for BB that humid night in the South of France. But it did lead to her making a radical reassessment of her life. And, as her long-time friend, film producer Christine Gouze-Renal revealed, it marked the emergence of a new Brigitte Bardot. 'Suicides,' said Mme Gouze-Renal, 'do not happen in twenty-four hours. They are a culmination of the way we are forced to live. People everywhere in the world have an ambivalent attitude towards Brigitte. They hate her and love her at the same time. She felt she was going mad and so she tried to end it. The attempted suicide awakened her to many things, made her more maternal to Nicolas, to responsibilities, to her world, to other people. She will never try it again.'

Brigitte Bardot had emerged from a dark tunnel. In the months and years which were to follow she would come to terms with being two people – Mlle Bardot, a quiet, complex yet uncertain woman; and BB, the screen's great sex symbol and idol of the permissive generation.

Below: The spot where Brigitte attempted suicide, pointed out by Jean-Louis Bournos, who found her. *Right*: Her wrists still bandaged, Brigitte leaves the Saint François Clinic in Nice

1961
The Bardot Myth

IN THE IMMEDIATE aftermath of her suicide attempt, Brigitte returned to *La Madrague*, and for once the press and the local people allowed her a winter of comparative peace and quiet. Perhaps a sense of mutual guilt at having created a superstar and then nearly destroyed her was at the bottom of a swell of feeling that arose from the French nation. Both factions had played a part in generating what had been the most traumatic year of the young woman's life, and the outcome had evidently had almost as deep an effect on the nation as on BB herself.

Bardot-watcher Gerard Fairlie summed up the feelings of many people at the turn of the year, when he wrote a perceptive article entitled, 'The Tragedy of Being a Sex Symbol'. 'The whole world,' he said, 'is waiting, for the most part with anxious sympathy, for news of Brigitte Bardot. Will she ever recover from the acute depression which has struck her down? She has to recover the will to live. If anyone can,' added Fairlie, 'she can.'

Late in January, it was announced that Brigitte was putting her troubles behind her and returning to the studios to make a light-hearted comedy, *La Bride Sur Le Cou* (retitled *Please Not Now!* in Britain and *Only For Love* in America) in which she played a lively model girl out to make her neglectful lover jealous. It was a role very much in the same mould as the Chouchous and Babettes of the earlier movies. Work was the way to recover her peace of mind, she decided. However, the film soon ran into trouble when Brigitte found herself unable to get on with Jean Aurel, the director, and with her contractual power of veto she had him taken off the picture. To replace Aurel she called on Roger Vadim – who, incidentally, had been quick to go to her side when news of the suicide attempt reached him. Vadim took over the film quickly and skilfully, later explaining his approach to *Variety* magazine:

'There wasn't a chance to polish lines or anything,' Vadim said. 'The comedy situations were made up right on the set because they seemed funnier than in the script. It gave us a great deal of spontaneity. I don't think we've ever made such a comedy in France before. French audiences love Hollywood slapstick, it's done with a great deal of skill, but French directors usually get their laughs from dialogue. With us, the lines must be funny. That's the theatrical tradition and it requires a kind of rigid logic that is very inhibiting.

'I am trying something that I have never done before and that is quite alien to the French cinema. That is situation comedy. Actually there isn't very much dialogue in the picture. You see I am quite convinced

111

that we French can be every bit as funny as the Americans if we permit ourselves to let loose.'

Roger Vadim was certainly able to get Brigitte to 'let loose' and the gossip that leaked out of the tightly-guarded Billancourt Studios was of a happy star getting on well with everybody around her. In a typical Vadim move, he gave her the name Sophie in the picture and set up a special dance sequence in which Brigitte appeared to offer a moment of full-frontal nudity. In truth she was wearing a diaphanous body-stocking – but the sequence was startling enough to run into trouble with the censors in both Britain and America. In Britain fifteen minutes of the picture had to be removed before it could be publicly shown, and in America the distributors, 20th Century Fox, had to fight with customs for some weeks to get their print cleared – and even then had to take a few minutes of screen time out.

Hearing of the British ban, Brigitte delivered one of her few accusing statements towards the country which had first discovered her. 'It's not a good thing to ban,' she declared. 'Banning just encourages curiosity and increases temptation. You don't stop children from smoking by banning it – they'll respond by smoking in secret. Far better to discourage them. Offer them a cigar or a pipe – they won't want to try again after the first puff. And it's the same with the cinema. For instance, I've never taken drugs, but if I had the desire to do so, just seeing the film *More* would have cured me of it.'

At the same time Brigitte's husband, the unhappy Jacques Charrier was accepting that he had now reached a point of no return. His marriage had crumbled and his wife clearly preferred the actor Sami Frey, who had remained in close attendance during the dramas of the previous few months. But Charrier did not come across as a bitter man when he spoke to the press.

'My marriage was a mistake,' he said quietly. 'But a mistake I'd like to make again. Unfortunately, I've found you can't have to yourself what titillates a whole nation – whether it's Bardot or Camembert!' And he added, 'We are on quite good terms, but that does not mean I have breakfast with her and Sami Frey.'

Brigitte had also apparently come to terms with both her parents and her son, Nicolas, as Willi Frischauer has reported: 'In spite of Brigitte's interests, views and lifestyle being diametrically opposed to those of her parents, she remained a – how shall we say – dutiful daughter. The older Bardots took turns with Jacques Charrier's parents looking after their grandchild, and it was touching to see Pilou spoon-feeding Nicolas ("Petit Pilou"). Brigitte forgave her father for his frequent outbursts about her behaviour and the reactions she provoked. She sensed his deep affection beneath the futile outrage and suspected that in spite of himself he was really proud of her fame. In the early sixties he presented her with a slim volume of poems of which she was the principal subject. "I have been writing for her since she was a baby," he said. They were stilted and gooey and made her wince, but she accepted the tribute with a white lie: "Most enjoyable" was her public comment. Pilou could not deny himself a mild rebuke in at least one of the verses:

Pretty, light shepherdess, I think you exaggerate
Lover, husband, children are not enough for you,
You need yet another lover, a respectable one, you say
And still you run around the night clubs
Oh! Shepherdess, you darling daredevil.

For a while, however, the little Shepherdess did not run around nightclubs but busied herself commissioning a new wing for her St. Tropez home, redecorating the farmhouse at Bazoches where Nicolas spent much of his time and, following the parting from Jacques Charrier, looking for a new and perhaps more palatial apartment in Paris. She found this in the Rue du Bac, and paid half a million Swiss francs for a top floor flat with an enormous private terrace where she could sunbathe undisturbed in the nude. It also had a marvellous view of the city which caused Brigitte to enthuse that she now had 'Paris at my feet'. This was certainly true in more ways than one! She also acquired a chalet at Meribel in the French Alps which she called *Le Chouan*, where she has since spent many winter holidays.

During the spring, Brigitte was briefly involved in filming one of the sketches in an anthology film, *Les Amours Célèbres*, directed by Michel Boisrond, which brought together a number of top French stars. BB played opposite the heart-throb Alain Delon in the 'Agnes Bernauer' story of the wife of a Bavarian prince who is accused of witchcraft and sentenced to death by drowning.

Then, in June, Brigitte embarked on what was to prove her major project of the year — not to mention one of her biggest films — a picture entitled *Vie Privée* (*Private Life*) which was immediately headlined as being a thinly-disguised version of her own life. Producer of the movie, which was to be shot in Paris, Geneva and the Italian city of Spoleto, was Brigitte's faithful friend, Christine Gouze-Renal, with one of the most exciting of the French 'new wave' film-makers, Louis Malle, as director.

Variety greeted the announcement of the project breathlessly on 12 April: 'The prospect of directing Brigitte Bardot in a motion picture in which she would attempt to portray Brigitte Bardot, the private woman and the public personality, might faze almost anybody else but Louis Malle. In the course of a short visit to New York last week, Malle reported that his friends had warned him against his upcoming project presently called *La Vie Privée* but bearing no relation to the Noël Coward bonbon. The picture, using Simone de Beauvoir's study of BB as a jumping-off point, will be financed by Metro.

'So far, so good,' said Malle, whose US reputation is based principally on his controversial paen to love (romantic and physical), *The Lovers*, as well as on his contributions as a writer, director and cameraman to Jacques Cousteau's *The Silent World*. One of the youngest (twenty-eight years old) and one of the most successful of France's 'new wave' directors, Malle said he had been told by friends that producer Christine Gouze-Renal would be interfering with his side of the project, but that until now, anyway, she had given him free rein and he anticipated no problems. BB, too, he said, had been a doll, but she was not yet completely convinced that they should go so far in *La Vie Privée* as to use her real name.

The Italian master of the sexy drama, Marcello Mastroianni, was selected to play Fabio, who turns an unspoiled country girl named Jill (Brigitte) on to the free-living and loving world of Paris where she rises from being an ordinary photographers' model to become Europe's highest paid sex-film actress. But unhappiness in the shape of frustrated love and constant harrassment by reporters greets her success and leads, ultimately, to tragedy.

113

The film naturally excited great interest among the public and the press were soon busy speculating on all the rumoured similarities to Brigitte's own life. It was not, however, until Louis Malle spoke out that the matter was put into perspective. In a lengthy interview with Andre Brunelin after shooting was finished he discussed the storyline and the difficulty of explaining the 'so-called myth of Brigitte Bardot.' (As this item has not been previously translated it will help clear up a number of misconceptions about the picture which still exist in the minds of non-French-speaking readers.)

'I am of the opinion that there is a lot about the parts she plays which has brought about Brigitte Bardot's sexual myth,' Malle began. 'However, I don't believe that it is a phenomenon that can be easily explained in a film. What interested me about *Vie Privée* was a fact of which I am quite certain: that Brigitte Bardot is a *Character*. I could not answer all the questions that are thrown up by this character, but some of them I can. You see, I believe that millions of people all over the world cannot be attracted to what she does without some foundation. Consequently, it was interesting to make a film with her, to allow her to play a part which corresponds so closely to her own.

'You can describe the film in the following way. For one and three-quarter hours, Brigitte is revealed to the public as she really is, although not without some artificial arrangement and recreation. Basically one sees the development of a person who, I think, comes rather close to what Bardot is really like.'

Malle went on to explain that in the film he had tried to show less of Brigitte Bardot's life and more of her character, which was what most fascinated him. 'The film certainly has something of the documentary about it,' he agreed. 'BB is never out of our vision, the camera is always directed at her. But it shows that her character is, contrary to many other views, one of extraordinary depth.

'At the start we all asked ourselves – who is this girl? Every day things are written about her, sometimes in praise of her and sometimes against. It looked as if it would be impossible to make a film about her. Would she in fact see it through? Or would it turn out to be phoney? And yet when we began work, there were days when she was staggeringly good, when she absolutely fascinated us. It was incredible. She really is an enigma! The success of the film, more than any other, lay squarely on her shoulders, and I think this proved that Brigitte is a star, quite unlike any other. If that were not so, we would certainly have ended up with a caricature of a person such as you see in *France Dimanche* or the like.'

Next Louis Malle turned to the specifics of *Vie Privée*. 'Basically, I think the film falls into three parts. The beginning in Geneva, which is of course before her fall into sin – that is the past. This part has a small insert which shows very briefly, through commentary and extracts from newspapers, her rise to fame. Then comes Paris, her success, and the confusion and the chaos which her life becomes. That is the present. The final part is a projection into the future – and is the most important part, I think.

'Imagine that BB, after a difficult and violent crisis, falls in love, and is in turn loved by someone who apparently has nothing in common with her. Who is a completely different kind of character and comes out of a different world. He hasn't the same interests as her, nor the same life.

114

This is Fabio, and it is through him that we got closer to understanding her. Fabio is an intellectual whose milieu is acting and the theatre. He is wrapped up in his work and like all people of that kind when he falls in love he cannot give up everything for it, neither can he sacrifice the one he loves. This is the point of departure in our film. Because it was then no longer autobiographical, we had all sorts of options open to us.

'Obviously the story could not end happily ever after. That can be felt right from the beginning. I am not against the principle of happy endings, but with this film it would have been completely senseless. Our end, a long fall into infinity, doesn't perhaps really mean death, it is a lyrical ending for a mythological heroine. You see, I like open endings. I could never have filmed the final scene with her lying completely shattered on the ground. And I am not really sure whether in the true sense of the word she dies. Perhaps it is only a part of her which falls away and dies, it's a little like a dream.

'All along we feel there is no way out for this romance. The more Brigitte is shut in, the more she shuts herself in. It would be naive to believe that this was all caused by other people, even the journalists – she herself carries part of the blame. Fabio's part shows the egoism of the creative being who is obsessed by his own career. Jill's great need is to be amongst people, an inclination that is even stronger in the real Brigitte. I believe we have shown a kind of ideal Bardot as she should be as well as she believes herself to be.'

Finally, Brunelin asked Louis Malle if he thought any other actress could have played the part of Jill.

'No, I don't think so,' he replied. 'The film draws too many elements from Brigitte's own life. I don't think anyone but her could have played those confrontations between herself and "herself", if I might express it like that, which occur later in the film. When she was acting those scenes she had to be in a state of great turmoil. Words sometimes exploded from her with incredible violence; yet at other times she was reserved and wonderfully sensitive. It was a quite astounding performance.'

Private Life remains an intriguing and revealing film, one of the most crucial in any study of BB and her life. The picture also represented another milestone in her career. For within days of completing it, she began to speak seriously for the first time about retiring from the screen . . .

Overleaf: 'Every man's dream . . .' Brigitte with Italian superstar Marcello Mastroianni in *A Very Private Affair*

1962
'A Woman of Sterling Qualities'

LOOKED AT TODAY, it is not difficult to understand how *Vie Privée* helped complete the renaissance of Brigitte's image with the general public. Believing the film to be literally true, they now felt they understood what her life had really been like behind the headlines, and how the pressures of stardom had driven her to the brink. Unlike Jill in the film, though, BB had been rescued by medical science and given another chance, and the public were determined that she should have a second chance at happiness.

There were still those who wished her ill, of course, but they were a minority. And an extraordinary attempt at blackmail helped win her more popularity. At Christmas she received a letter from the extreme right-wing French group, the OAS (Secret Army Organisation) demanding fifty thousand new francs to help fight 'the *de facto* power of Monsieur de Gaulle', who was then, of course, the President.

When Brigitte took this demand to the police, lodging a complaint of 'attempted blackmail and extortion', there were misgivings that it was nothing more than a publicity stunt. Not satisfied, she sent a copy to the left-wing weekly newspaper, *L'Express* which reprinted the letter complete with its signature 'for General Raoul Salan, commander-in-chief of the OAS —

J. Lenoir, head of financial services'. The missive was a duplicated sheet headed by the words 'Secret Army Organisation – Metropolitan Zone – Headquarters' on which Brigitte's name and address and the sum she was being asked to pay (equivalent to £3,700) were typewritten. The money, said the letter, was to help the OAS fight not only de Gaulle but also the Communists and the Algerian FLN (National Liberation Front).

Enquiries by the newspaper showed that businessmen and other well-known individuals in the Paris region had received similar demands. In a defiant statement to *L'Express* Brigitte said, 'I won't pay because I have no wish to live in a Nazi country.' She added that the OAS would be quickly put down if it was met with a blunt and public refusal 'from the people they are trying to terrorise by their threats and attacks'.

De Gaulle himself responded to her stand. 'This young woman seems to be made of sterling qualities,' he said in a statement that – for him – was fulsome in its praise.

Writing of this episode, Willi Frischauer has said, 'Her brave action threw light on the extent of the rackets, some political, some plain criminal, which harassed leading French men and women. To guard Brigitte against OAS revenge, a policeman was posted outside her house. At the studio, her beloved mongrel Guapa was kept in "protective custody" while she joined film workers at a protest rally and, her fist raised high, swore to fight fascism to the death. Threats continued and there was a vague but disturbing hint that the OAS gangsters were planning to abduct little Nicolas and hold him to ransom. Brigitte dropped everything and took the boy to Switzerland until matters had cooled down. But she did not compromise.'

This prompt and courageous action – at least one of the recipients of a similar letter was later injured by an OAS *bombe-plastique* –was the first sign of her new sense of responsibility. Her first identification with a cause she believed in, and proof of her willingness to stand up and be counted regardless of the consequences. They were certainly not the actions of an empty-headed sex symbol. Nor were they to be her last.

On 5 February Brigitte returned to the secure surroundings of the studios to make what was to prove her only film of the year, *Le Repos du Guerrier* (retitled *Warrior's Rest* for the British cinema and *Love On a Pillow* in America). Roger Vadim was again the man at the helm with darkly handsome Robert Hossein as the neurotic, drunken nihilist who turns Brigitte, a *petit bourgeois*, into a liberated though not necessarily happy woman. The territory was a familiar one for Vadim, and was based on a prize-winning novel of the same title by one of his friends, Christiane Rochefort. Before filming began he was quick, as usual, with a statement of intent.

'What really interests me in the relationship between a man and woman,' he said, 'is their language. In *Et Dieu Créa la Femme* it was the language of a girl; in *Sait-On Jamais*, the language of a boy. *Le Repos du Guerrier* is the language of a couple. The film gives me the opportunity of illustrating one of my theories that man is abstract and woman concrete: to determine to what point man can reject the laws of society and still survive.'

Talk of freedom in various forms was to dominate the making of this picture through the next two months – and then explode in April when Brigitte confirmed what the gossips had been whispering for months:

'This is my last film,' she announced as it drew to a close. 'I promised Vadim I'd do it. *Ma décision est ir-ré-vo-ca-ble. Après Le Repos du Guerrier, le repos de Brigitte.*' It was already widely known that her earnings from films had topped the one million pounds mark – but this did not explain her decision. So why quit?

'I haven't found anything good in the scripts I've been shown lately,' she replied, 'but even if I had I wouldn't have accepted. In life it is sometimes necessary to step back. I've been filming for ten years without a pause. I need to get my bearings.'

There were those among her audience who listened without conviction – and as time proved, those misgivings were well-founded – but the announcement generated headlines around the world, as well as profiles on her life as high-flown and often inaccurate as so much that had already been written. Arguably only one really perceptive essay emerged from this 'retirement' announcement, written by Jean Cau, the

Brigitte with her 'Victoire' – the French equivalent of the 'Oscar' – awarded to her in 1959

120

Prix Goncourt-winning French novelist who was later to join with Roger Vadim to script another of Brigitte's controversial films, *Don Juan 1973*. It was published, appropriately, in *L'Express*, and Cau began by asking her if it was true – as reported – that she rarely read anything written about herself:

'"If by chance I do read some of it," she replied, "I become demoralised. It is always the same. None of it is true."

'"What is true then?"

'"I don't know myself. I don't know what the truth about me is. But I do know, when I read these things, what the lies are."

'We fell silent. Then I launched out into an odd speech. I explained that – whether one was called Stalin, Napoleon, de Gaulle or Bardot – it was almost the same thing from a certain point of view. You climb, step by step, to the heights of fame. As you rise, the air becomes rarefied, the vision gets blurred, you feel giddy, and when you are there, on top of the pyramid, you are alone. Isn't this true?

'"Oh, yes, that's the terrible thing," she said. "Yes, indeed . . . I have perhaps four or five friends in all. My true friends are the ones I had when I was a girl."

'She longs to be a member of the ordinary crowd. But, like a pack of hounds, they devour her, tear her to pieces – or sell her. The hounds are ready to pounce.

'"I have been given everything, but I cannot make use of the gifts. And time is passing and I am fettered, a prisoner behind my own face."

'The myth, then, is this: a ravishing child-woman who is afraid and who must cry out in sorrow when she is alone; whose sadness periodically rises to a climax when she no longer understands it.

'She tells me (still calm, and I can almost see the firm little core under that golden helmet) that she is permanently in a state of anxiety. When she no longer understands her life she wants to break it, as a child wants to break a toy which is too complicated.

'"Yet," she confesses, "I am afraid of death, very much afraid. Because I do not like ugly things. But in moments of great anguish I should like to slip out of it. There is that door which I long to open . . .

'"I have had many lovers in my life. It has been said that I am wicked. But it is not a matter of wickedness, it is a matter of affection or tenderness.

'"For me, the only existence which counts – besides my own – is that of a man. But which man?

'"I don't see anybody: I live in a very small circle. The same people come and go, as on a merry-go-round. So, when I am very depressed, when I feel like drowning, I clutch at any support, the nearest at hand. But as I get older I pull myself together: I try to cope by myself."

'And do you succeed?

'"Not quite, no . . . no woman ever does . . ."

'Her profession, she tells me, no longer interests her. That has become a matter of big money and of publicity. The fame she did not desire.

'"I never wanted anything," she said. "It just happened. I never would have believed it. Now it has swallowed me up. It's all business. In the beginning, it is a pleasant sensation to win the first prize. Now . . ."

'But it is not embarrassing to project one's body on the cinema screen . . .?

'"Not for me . . . There's nothing indecent about it. The dirtiness is in the minds of people who see it that way. I never made a film in tucked-up skirts, suspenders and black stockings . . . That is hypocritical obscenity . . .

'"Now, quite obviously, I have become imprisoned in an image. Even if I were to play a nun, you know what the posters would be like . . . That is why I have had enough of it and why I'm giving up."

'No more cinema? After *Le Repos du Guerrier*, will it all be over? Well! I can see a producer jumping over the wall of the garden where you grow your roses. And he'll tap his briefcase and he'll say . . . "Here you are, 400,000,000 francs!" And then Eurydice Bardot will close her eyes and follow the new Orpheus.

'"No." she says firmly. "First of all I've already been offered those 400,000,000 francs. And then I've been rejecting all offers for the past two years. For two years I have refused to sign any contract. Offers have become bigger and bigger and more and more numerous.

'"What am I to do with the money? I don't like jewels, furs, parties . . . I have a horror of the big couturiers. You come out of their places looking a fright."

'You are said to be appallingly stingy. (She doesn't flinch. Full marks for self-control.)

'"Why do I want to stop then?" she goes on, "Why do I refuse all this filthy lucre? I don't know what I've got in the bank, I swear. My agent sees to the accounts. I have nothing to do with them. I don't care.

'"I tell you that one of my pleasures is to give – even to people I don't know. But I don't throw money right and left; I find that stupid and vulgar. I don't give outrageous cocktail parties and I don't invite two hundred people at a time: it bores me and it is silly.

'"Granted, even if I do earn millions, it

still gives me pleasure to be paid fifty thousand francs for a little something I do. I am happy. They pay me for the little thing, that's nice and quite normal."

'I mark time. Then I say, Have you been pulling my leg ever since I came here? Did you put on a show to deceive me? A dialogue, you know, is more or less a trial of strength. Which of us is trying to lead the other by the nose? You?

'"No," she says, "not at all . . . If only you knew how much of a sham I feel . . . There are days when I feel absolutely rotten and I find myself cheap and showy all the time. That's why I don't go out.

'"People imagine they are going to see the seventh wonder of the world: but if I don't put on a mink and a hat, you should hear what they say. It depresses me. And I have no confidence in myself anyway."

'And what does she think of fame, her fame?

'"If I were only what they say I am, empty-headed, with a bird's brain and all that – I should be a nobody."

'What is the source of your fame then?

'"By now it keeps going on its own impetus."

'But at the start?

'"In spite of being feeble and exploited, I believe that I have a certain strength. Strength of character. I don't run away. I commit myself. Then I have a certain talent for organisation. And, finally, willpower." (She is silent and reflects, biting her lip.)

'"What I dislike is superficiality. I hate it – and I am a superficial person myself. Consequently my fame, as you call it, rests on air and – to a great extent – on hate. There are people who hate me . . ."

'Tell me. She does. She speaks of the women who in the streets treat her like a slut and accuse her of having soiled the world: of the men who treat her like a tart and ask her either to clear out or to display her charms.

'She speaks of the spectre of the Devil and of the Witch which the combined forces of lewdness and virtue will bring to the stake (naked of course) in some public place. Even so, fame continues.

'"I don't care about that," she continues. "Perhaps a girl like Jayne Mansfield loves it. I don't. But I'm sure that the anxiety which I drag about with me will vanish when all that causes it vanishes."

'Well, so you will have a pink house with green shutters, a husband, children, neighbours . . .?

'"No, not that kind of life . . ."

'What other life, then?

'"Another job. It doesn't matter what. I must keep busy and I must have a real life," she added.'

Good as her word, Brigitte *did* drop out of public view once work on *Le Repos du Guerrier* was complete. For much of the rest of the year she lived a secluded, carefree existence in St. Tropez with Sami Frey by her side. Their affair apparently endured because it was a case of opposites attracting one another. 'It is true that it is painful to live with me,' she remarked at the end of the year. 'I am expensive, I laugh, I play, I dance. Sami is the opposite. He is afraid, he suffers, he is hypersensitive.'

From her sun-kissed eyrie, *La Madrague*, she also expressed delight when her favourite film, *La Vérité*, carried off the European *Grand Prix du Cinema*; and at the news that she had been voted Favourite Female Actress in polls in four different countries (France, Belgium, Austria and Switzerland). There was pleasure, too, at the announcement that *Le Repos du Guerrier* had opened in Paris during the week of her

twenty-eighth birthday to the highest box office takings in French cinema history.

The past twelve months had certainly worked a miraculous change in Brigitte's life. But if she – or the world – imagined that calmer times lay ahead, both were in for a big surprise.

Brigitte reunited with Roger Vadim yet again for
Warrior's Rest. Her co-star was Robert Hossein

1963
Riots in London!

BRIGITTE'S 'RETIREMENT' IN 1962 created, if anything, an even bigger public interest in her work and her legend. Magazine and newspaper stories proliferated – though noticeably without any new quotes from the subject – while her films continued to dominate the world's cinema screens. Pictures from her earlier days were hastily snapped up by distributors on both sides of the Atlantic and, often provocatively retitled, fed the public demand for BB in any shape or form. Even if her role was minor, her acting amateur and all her clothes stayed on, it seemed to matter not a bit.

A survey estimated that over twenty-five thousand pin-up photographs of her had been published, and that as France's most famous export she was worth more to the national exchequer than any other single item – the ever-popular Renault cars included. It was also reported from America that several universities were busy collecting material on the Bardot phenomenon, and to cap it all a Soviet diplomat, returning home from Europe, was arrested at Moscow Airport and charged with attempting to smuggle three thousand photographs of Brigitte in various states of nudity into the country!

In January, Brigitte travelled up from the South of France for a brief reunion with her husband Jacques Charrier. They met in Paris to bring to an end their marriage, and after going through the obligatory appearance before a divorce judge to see if there was any hope of reconciliation, the formalities were completed in a Paris civil court. The couple filed a cross petition which alleged 'serious insults'.

The parting was amicable enough, both having previously agreed on the terms of the settlement. There was no quarrel over their son, Nicolas. Custody was given to Jacques Charrier, while Brigitte was granted the right to have him with her for six months each year. She had never made any secret of her lack of maternal instinct, but nevertheless she loved and cherished her child and has always continued to do so.

Then back into seclusion she went with Sami Frey – until April, when one of the most dynamic new talents to emerge on the French cinema scene came calling with a rather special film project. The man was Jean-Luc Godard, doyen of *La Nouvelle Vague*, and his film was *Le Mépris* (*Mistrust*), based on a novel by one of the grand old men of European literature, Alberto Moravia. It was a challenging package bulging with class, and Brigitte found it impossible to resist.

The return of BB to the screen naturally attracted American film-makers, and Joe

Levine's Avco-Embassy Pictures put up the money to finance the picture. As long – they insisted – as they got BB in the nude. To co-star with Brigitte, Godard cast a heavyweight American actor with box-office appeal as great as her own, Jack Palance. The picture was to be filmed in Capri and Rome. The storyline concerned a down-at-heel hack writer (played by Michael Piccoli) who is given a chance to refurbish his reputation and finances by writing part of the script for an epic version of *The Odyssey* being filmed in Italy. Taking his wife (BB) along with him, he soon finds himself enmeshed in the problems of an un-workable script and a growing attraction between his wife and the film's ruthless pro-ducer, played by Jack Palance.

Brigitte vividly expressed her excitement about the project. 'I've joined the new wave now,' she said. 'Godard was really scared, you know. Me, too. He came to see me; we call each other Monsieur Godard and Mademoiselle Bardot. He watched me serve tea – he said he had to get to know me as I really am. Later, he wouldn't say any-thing at all.'

Godard, who had always delighted in clothing his work in rhetoric, went to some lengths in an interview in *Le Monde* to explain the significance of Brigitte's nude scenes ('I wanted to transfigure her, because the cinema can and must trans-figure reality'). He did, though, manage to encapsulate his theme in these words: 'A fleeting feeling of the vanity of things, all that happens and is of no importance. All this in a space well-defined by the Odyssey, the sea, the Mediterranean sun, etc. It is the rapport of these concrete realities with something indeterminate.'

Making the picture in Italy naturally attracted the attentions of those most per-sistent photographers, the *paparazzi*. No matter how hard Brigitte tried to avoid their intrusive lenses they were never far away, a group of them even going to the length of hiring a helicopter to hover over the apartment block where she was living. The main purpose of their mission, apparently, was to discover whether, as she was appearing in the film with black hair, she had actually dyed those famous golden locks in an attempt to get away from her old image – or if she was just wearing a wig. (It was, of course, a wig.)

An astute French film-maker, Jacques Rozier, who happened to be both a friend of Godard and a member of the *nouvelle vague*, had the bright idea of making a film about the relentless pursuit of Bardot by the photographers. Granted access to the sets and moving around BB as she dodged the cameramen, he put together a short but fas-cinating film which he called *Paparazzi*. Sadly never released outside France, the picture is a striking documentary of the relationship between the film stars (in this case Brigitte, Michael Piccoli and Jean-Luc Godard) and the cameramen, a relation-ship mingling love and hate and an impressive display of inventiveness on both sides.

As more than one critic has pointed out, *Paparazzi* went some way to explaining why Brigitte had come out of 'retirement'. It showed that she would have the utmost dif-ficulty finding the privacy she craved even if she *did* give up work, because there was no way the press or the public would ever leave her alone. In truth, she was better pro-tected behind the closed doors of a studio or on an out-of-bounds location than living in her Paris flat or South of France home. At the end of May, Brigitte finally escaped the clutches of the *paparazzi* and returned to

France, where new film offers now awaited her. She could hardly have dreamed that a still more hectic foreign encounter awaited her that same year.

For the first time in several years, Brigitte attended the Cannes Film Festival and despite the determined efforts of a number of starlets to pull the same stunt that had originally enabled her to capture the attention of the world's photographers (several went topless and two quite naked), BB still emerged as the sexiest 'Queen of the Screen'. And on the verge of her twenty-ninth birthday this was no mean achievement in an industry obsessed with youth. The Festival also brought another man into her life. During the festivities she met a dark-haired, handsome and intelligent Brazilian named Bob Zaguri, who described himself as a wealthy motor car dealer. He became a constant companion, and was by her side throughout the extraordinary events which engulfed her in London in October.

For her second film after 'retirement', Brigitte decided on another change of pace, playing a lady's maid in an out-and-out farce called *Une Ravissante Idiote* (which has been variously retitled *A Ravishing Idiot*, *Adorable Idiot* and *Bewitching Scatterbrain*). Starring with her was Anthony Perkins, an actor for whom she had expressed admiration. Perkins played a young Russian spy living it up in capitalist London, who recruits Brigitte to help him steal some highly secret documents in the possession of her employer's husband.

Although most of the filming was scheduled for the Studios Billancourt, producer Michel Ardan decided on adding a little authenticity by including some actual location work in London. So Brigitte found herself in the Westbury Hotel, just off Bond Street, in late October. Almost immediately the hotel was besieged by fans, who outnumbered the normal posse of press photographers by fifty to one. Seeing the crowds, Brigitte expressed an understandable concern. 'Why are they all here?' she asked – as if she couldn't guess. Bob Zaguri did his best to calm her during the tense hours which followed as the crowd showed no signs of dispersing. Then, when she went

Brigitte with Jack Palance, her co-star in *Mistrust* (1963)

to the first location spot, Flask Walk in Hampstead, on the afternoon of Friday, 23 October, things really boiled over. Michael Blakey, a journalist on the *Daily Express*, who was present at the time, describes what happened:

'Hundreds of people crowded the set in Flask Walk as BB arrived in chauffeur-driven elegance. But most were so keen to get a close-up of BB's statistics that filming had to be cancelled.

'Trouble started at four o'clock when France's best known export arrived to film scenes for the French thriller *Adorable Idiot*.

'But photographers, hanging out of windows, and fans trying to get in on the set brought filming to an end in uproar. And as an angry Bardot left for her hotel, French film producer Michel Ardan, who had pleaded with Bardot admirers, said: "That's it. We will not film in England. Back to France . . ."'

Brigitte retreated to her room at the Westbury Hotel (number 501) and spoke briefly to a small coterie of journalists. 'Will I ever be able to make a film in London?' she wondered. 'It couldn't happen in Paris – there people accept me. I have never known anything quite like this before, it was very frightening.'

Later, safely back in France, Brigitte was able to talk more calmly about an event that had clearly upset her, and marked her yet again as a star unlike any other. Sophia Loren, Gina Lollobrigida, Jayne Mansfield, even Marilyn Monroe had been able

Opposite: A chat with fans in Flask Walk Hampstead. *Above:* Despite the problems, *Adorable Idiot* is finished, much to the relief of the cast

to come to London and film street scenes without creating a riot among fans. Not, though, BB. She told reporters:

'I am terrified of crowds. They fill me with fear and that is difficult because by all the laws of our profession, a star is expected to live in the glare of publicity surrounded by a vast public. For me this is a special strain. I was not brought up to it. I did not seek it. I do not want it. It is almost impossible for me to lead an ordinary life. If I go to the theatre I have to slip in at a side entrance. If I go to a restaurant other people stare. The meal is ruined. Yet I have no wish to do an "act" by hiding. I just want to live as a woman, not as an actress. It is for that reason that I rarely appear in public. Mind you, when I fail to appear at a gala I am sometimes accused of spoiling the show simply because I am not there. That is

unfair. I like lots of sleep, you see.'

Brigitte also parted the curtains a little on what she liked to do when she was at home. Potter about, for one thing, and play records. She also spent a lot of time with animals, she said, and hoped one day to campaign on behalf of certain threatened species. (She was to fulfill this objective with great dedication later on.)

'I adore animals, you see,' she went on, 'all animals except fish. I have two dogs, a spaniel and a cocker spaniel. I have six doves and ten love birds. Why, I even like mice and when my cat caught one recently I saved it but, alas, in spite of all my efforts the mouse died.'

Hastily, a number of sets representing various London locations were built in the Billancourt Studios, and Brigitte and Anthony Perkins got on with the business of completing the picture. It went down in film history as the first picture ever to be halted by fans, but it was not well received by critics. Margaret Hinxman of the *Daily*

131

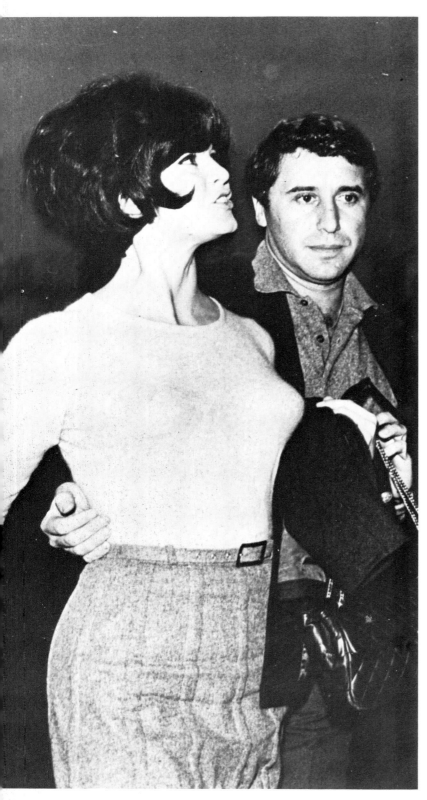

Cinema represented most opinions when she wrote, 'The plot is strictly Marxian (Groucho not Karl), but the treatment is something less than sprightly and the chatter a bit overbearing.' She was prepared to concede, though, that 'no film's ever found BB a handicap!'

Now that Brigitte had two films behind her since her abortive attempt to quit the business – and she showed every indication of being willing to consider more – offers poured in to her Paris agent. Aside from those for films, a nightclub owner in Florida tried to lure her across the Atlantic with an enormous offer to appear in cabaret. She would only go, she said, for a million dollars – and that was the end of that. But while this bartering went on, BB had three other things very much on her mind. One was that she did not want to get back into the rat-race of rushing from one film to the next without a break, as she had done before. Secondly, she wanted to spend more time with Bob Zaguri, who had been such a tower of strength during the debacle in London, and was urging her to go with him to his native Brazil to celebrate the Carnival season. And, thirdly, she was just about to embark on her thirtieth year . . .

Left: Brigitte with lover, Bob Zaguri, who rescued her from the crowds in London. *Opposite*: In disguise in *Viva Maria!*

132

1964
BB at Thirty

During 1964, for the first time in twelve years, Brigitte Bardot and the film camera did not share their customary love affair. With the exception of a week's work filming a New Year's Eve television spectacular, and a five-minute spot in *Dear Brigitte*, an American film about a little boy's dream of meeting her, Brigitte took the year off to be with Bob Zaguri. As ever, of course, cameras were around to record each passing day that she spent in public (and even some she did not).

In February the couple sped off to Brazil to share in the fun, music and gaiety which is Carnival. News of their impending arrival went ahead of them, and coupled with rumours that they were planning to marry, a real South American reception was planned by the romantically-inclined Brazilians. Thousands waited to greet them at Rio de Janeiro, and understandably Brigitte had fears of a repeat of the London scenes. Police had in fact to clear a way for her car to leave the airport, and large crowds milled around her hotel near Copacabana Beach for days afterwards.

Willi Frischauer who reported the events in Rio wrote, 'Bardot fever was not confined to Brazil's *hoi polloi*. The cabinet in session at the presidential palace opposite the hotel broke off and ministers tried to catch a glimpse of Brigitte. I depend on a Brazilian observer – perhaps not too reliable – as a source of the information that, for the following three days, the wife of President Goulard stood at her window armed with a telescope in the hope of seeing "*la grande Bébé*." There were, literally, no two ways about the traffic chaos in the Copacabana as motorists stopped and stared. Fifty armed soldiers guarded the hotel against invasion.'

Brigitte and Bob did, though, manage to slip out and join in the Carnival processions. Disguised, of course – Zaguri as a king and BB in a suitably scanty costume and mask as 'the King's slave'. Although much of the furore over her visit died down after a week, Brigitte still found it necessary to hide behind dark glasses and a hat (sometimes even a dark wig) whenever the couple went out. This she was able to abandon when they left the capital and spent four months travelling through the lush jungle country or lazing on the eye-dazzling strands of silver beaches which are strung along the coastline.

When the couple reluctantly dragged themselves away from this life of lotus-

BB relaxing with Bob Zaguri off the coast of Brazil

eating and returned to France, it was on the eve of Brigitte's thirtieth birthday. To celebrate, she held a small party at *La Madrague*, which her sister, Mijanou, attended. along with a few other close friends. She blew out thirty candles on a large birthday cake and ruminated on what this particular birthday meant. Her words were later relayed by Anthony Perkins:

'The ideal age is my age. At my age one is old enough to know what one is doing and young enough to do it all the same. I am thirty, but there are things about me that are still fifteen. I have gone through much in my life and yet I do not feel that I have suffered great tragedies. I love to love and I hate to leave, but I love freely and I leave freely.'

Later she was to add to this: 'I wonder why everyone makes such a song and dance about thirty? Certainly it is a milestone. But I do not feel all that changed. I would be sad if I had remained the way I was ten years ago. But make no mistake – although I have calmed down it does not mean I have become a stick-in-the-mud. I am now sensitive to a lot of things I never felt before. My feelings can be touched by injustice, poverty, sickness, treason – and suffering.'

Such a landmark as the thirtieth birthday of a woman who was now a legend and a French institution could not be allowed to pass without comment in the national press – or in the press of the rest of the world. The accolades flew thick and fast – there *were* brickbats, too – but that Brigitte gave them more than a cursory glance is highly unlikely. As she felt disinclined to give special interviews, the profiles were for the most part re-hashes of what had been written before.

An exception to this, was an article by one of the leading French literary authors,

Marguerite Duras (scriptwriter of the famous film *Hiroshima, Mon Amour*), who chose to look at BB through the medium of her photographs. As arguably the most photographed women of our times, it was a novel approach to the subject, and though certain of Mme Duras' observations may be open to dispute, does make for a unique portrait of the star at thirty.

'I have been looking closely at some photographs of Brigitte Bardot taken this summer,' Mme Duras wrote. 'Something has happened to this woman. Certainly her body, though a trifle less well moulded inside her golden skin, still remains superb. But in her face something has frozen. A slight painful puckering of the mouth and the eyes, which yesterday was not there. Yesterday, facing the world, this face was majestically carefree. Today, she keeps a close watch on it. That is the difference – her pose. In other words, fear. Is this the end of a dazzling morning? Of course not – but already the warning signs of evening are here. An evening full of wolves.

'As a shapely girl of sixteen it must have happened to her very naturally. She must have gone out into the street and the first man to see her – who already had a foothold in the cinema – noticed her. She did not go forward to meet her career. The mountain came to her. And she experienced the eternity of beauty and, yes, the fun of youth. Then one day she must have discovered she was twenty-one. And then twenty-five. I think that around this triumphal age she must have glimpsed the greatest test which man has been given to live through – that of growing old. It seems it was at that very age that Bardot was found unconscious one night on the Côte d'Azur. She came back to continue what she had begun: love and films. And now today the absurdly impossible has come to pass: Brigitte, our little girl, has reached the incredible age of thirty.

'However much of a paradox it may seem, I believe nothing has happened to Bardot between the time she began to act and today. Nothing, neither the love of a man nor that of her little boy Nicolas. Not even the fleeting wonder of motherhood. One cannot alone create opportunities to forget oneself and squander one's energy. Somebody else is necessary. Somebody else? I believe Bardot does not know this. Did she ever know? Perhaps. But until now nobody has known what lies inside this immense and sumptuous strong-box.

'Time passes with impunity over both empty and well-filled lives. Whether or not it has all been worth it, some time, some summer, some day, everything is covered by the same shroud. Scarcely six years separate Brigitte from Jeanne Moreau. But they are an abyss. One day Jeanne took her age in her hands, studied it carefully and told it: "Let's make a deal. I shall become

less and less young – that's only fair. But you must never again catch me unawares."

'Personally, I am a little apprehensive about Bardot. Reckless, lazy, dragging herself through countless love affairs, such is Bardot, our little girl. We watched her grow up and we would so much wish her to round that unavoidable bend of thirty years this month as safely as possible, without suffering, with self-control and with forethought. Indeed the whole of France is agog. For we love her. All the French highbrows are on her side. As for the public at large, they are split between the men who are all in love with her and the women who, sometimes, accept her. But Bardot teams up with nobody, at least with no set. The highbrows' friendship does not seem to be

A brief appearance for BB in the film which concerned a small boy's infatuation with her, *Dear Brigitte* (1956). Co-stars James Stewart and Billy Mumy look suitably impressed

mutual. Above all she likes people who amuse or interest her. For instance, the public jesters of the St. Tropez bars, the lonely, homesick and charming young men from every walk of life.

'She is basically lonely, absolutely on her own, at the head of a team which does not exist. In her private life she is very bored. She trails around her various homes, decorated by up-to-date antique dealers, with no idea of how to spend her time. Nature has happily endowed her with a delicious talent for idleness. But this is not enough to kill time. So she invents childish games to shake off her boredom. She receives few visitors. She lives alone with her lover so long as she is in love with him. I am certain that she has never known the end of a love affair, the heartbreaking depression of loneliness and liberty. But she knows that other tragedy of starting afresh right away. Has she ever paused between two romances – got her second wind – has she ever done this? I don't think so. Her will is strong. Nobody has ever broken the toy. Any woman would be the same if someone had "irreparably wronged her by loving her too much". So says a man who lived a year with her.

'"She is so beautiful, so extraordinarily desirable at every moment of her life, all hours of the day and night, whatever her mood, whether she is gay, sad or bored. She is so desirable that life with her becomes an inferno of desire. One cannot hesitate to approach her, to pester her, to live in terror of losing her. I think all her men have exhausted her patience. I, too . . . it's enough to drive a man mad. I was mad throughout the period we lived together."

'When a man attracts her, Bardot goes straight to him. Nothing stops her. It does not matter if she is in a café, at home or staying with friends. She goes off with him on the spot without a glance at the man she is leaving. In the evening perhaps she will come back – or perhaps not. Thus this woman who has never been forsaken does not understand – among many other things – the atrociousness of her behaviour. Although she has left many corpses in her wake she herself remains unharmed. This is what I mean when I say that nothing has ever happened to her yet.

'From this sublime body in its most glorious vigour a child was made. But no miracle was wrought. No doubt because she no longer had sufficient love for the man who had fathered it. But also because she did not have the means to behave like a real mother to the child who would have become a rival. It seems strange. She wants to be alone and independent. But alone in a bed she is prey to such great anguish that she cannot sleep. She needs somebody to lull her to sleep, to be her companion. Our adorable little girl is a child even in her elementary notion of solitude. The sleep of her lover is her sleep. I don't say that this is selfishness, no. I'm saying something quite different – that Bardot is a mythological being even in her own eyes. Each of her lovers is in some degree a night-duty man, the person who will enable her to avoid sleeping alone. The curious thing, nevertheless, is that although all have been warned of the danger of loving her nobody has yet recoiled.

'It is not out of spite that I speak like this of our idol. People often talk about her but rarely seriously. She deserves that now and then somebody should talk of her power and mystery without lying. She makes me think of a little tightrope walker I met one day who could not remember the first time he climbed on to the highwire. So he knew

138

nothing of the anguish of learning to do so, nor – worse still – of other people's fears for him.

'I am sorry that nothing more important has happened to Bardot than to be our idol; that a very, very strong wind never encountered before has not blown across her these last few years, that she has never committed a great and noble mistake. But how can this be averted, even if we wished it? One day she will discover that what is happening to her is neither more or less than the fate of all human beings and nothing else.'

So another landmark year had been reached in the remarkable life of Brigitte Bardot. She was thirty, still world-famous and still at the top of her profession. What did the future hold? Strangely, the events of 1964 already held the clues. Although she had resisted for so long flying the Atlantic, the past year had seen her visit South America for the first time. Early in the new year she was to return – to Mexico this time – to film with another of France's most beautiful stars, Jeanne Moreau, whom Marguerite Duras had chanced to mention in her profile – though she clearly had no foreknowledge of the partnership to come. More surprising still, Brigitte was at last to go of her own accord to the one place that for years had been unavailingly trying to lure her with all manner of blandishments and offers of money – the United States.

While in Brazil, Brigitte buys an apartment in the fashionable suburb of Rio de Janeiro, appropriately known as 'Enchanted Valley'

1965
The Conquest of America

THE NEXT MAN to tempt Brigitte back into filming was Louis Malle, who had directed her stunning performance in *Vie Privée*. He journeyed down to *La Madrague* during the winter months to put to Brigitte the idea of making a movie with France's other great screen beauty of the time, his protégée, Jeanne Moreau. It was a bold plan, because few other actors – male or female – were prepared to appear with Brigitte because they feared, quite rightly, that it was BB the audience's eyes would be on. But when it was two gorgeous women together, what then . . .?

Malle, who came from a wealthy French family and had to overcome the objections of his parents to become a film-maker, had first worked for Jacques Cousteau on *The Silent World*, and then made his reputation in *L'Ascenseur pour l'Echafaud* (*Lift to The Scaffold*) in 1957, which also made a star of the leading lady, Jeanne Moreau. His new project was to link BB and JM in a film entitled *Viva Maria!* based on a book *The Beautiful Blonde from Bashful Bend* by Preston Sturges, about a travelling circus that becomes involved in a turn-of-the-century revolution in Central America. The two girls formed a redoubtable partnership both as performers and later as revolutionaries – becoming national heroines in the process.

Brigitte read Louis Malle's script at a sitting and loved it. The idea of going to Mexico to film also appealed to Bob Zaguri, and so BB agreed to the proposal on the spot. She was not the least deterred by the thought of sharing top billing with Moreau, who was older (thirty-seven) and renowned as a very accomplished actress – although the announcement of the film naturally 'took the film world by surprise' according to the newspaper headlines which greeted it. BB set the record straight in an interview (her first in almost a year) given to the French radio station, Europe No. 1:

'This film with Jeanne is really going to be fun,' she said. 'It is a sort of burlesque comedy with music. I play an Irish anarchist in the 1914–18 war. I blow up bridges because my father is an anarchist.

'It is a fairly odd sort of story because Jeanne Moreau is a music-hall singer who is looking for a partner and we sing together through wars and revolutions.'

Did it worry her sharing the spotlight with another woman? 'Not at all – it delights me – I like Jeanne very much. Perhaps you might say we are two aspects of the ideal woman. I hardly knew her until the film was proposed, then we dined together, listened to songs together, and we hit it off immediately. It is thè first time I have accepted to play with another star of

141

the first rank. We will have exactly the same billing and that pleases me – it's such a change '

Does she undress? 'Yes, we undress as one did in 1914 – we lift our dresses to reveal a calf very slowly. That's what they called a striptease in those days. Wonderful!'

The location for shooting the film was the Mexican resort of Cuernavaca, and as soon as the two superstars were at work, Louis Malle knew his intuition that they had much in common and could spark each other off had not been mistaken.

'They are both very, very sensitive,' he said, 'and they have terrific sex appeal, though of a different kind. They feel always in danger, all the time they live on the edge of their nerves. I thought it would be funny to have Bardot and Moreau in the same picture. I wanted the chemistry between the trained actress and the film star, the sophisticated woman and the instinctive child.'

Peter Evans, the London journalist from the *Daily Express* who had charted much of Brigitte's early career, visited the set in February, not long after filming had got under way. He vividly described the conditions in which he found the film crew at work:

'It is a long drive from Mexico City, south through country the colour of scorched khaki. The roads squeeze through old, anonymous villages and out into the open, clouds of hot dust following you all the way. Through canyons of wolves and on between mountains with snow-peaks glinting in the sun. Past shawled and shrivelled women who were never young, and children who will never be old. It is a hard and beautiful land.

'It is here that two of the world's most fascinating women have come to film together for the first time. Brigitte Bardot and Jeanne Moreau. Two women who, in their strangely different styles, have emerged as aspects of the complete woman, the eternal female.'

Evans found Brigitte looking 'unbelievably good'. 'She has lost weight, but 'there is still that astonishing amalgam of early innocence and bold sexuality in her face.' He also found her more at peace with herself.

'You see I must think of myself first,' she told him. 'Is that selfish? Perhaps in a certain way, yes. But then I make up for my selfishness by spoiling others. I have always spoiled the men in my life. I like spoiled men around me because spoiled people are happy people. I spoil men and children and dogs. It is good to be surrounded by happy people. Anyway what is happy? Happiness is such a big word. I can be happy with simple things – beautiful sunsets, a rough sea, children playing.

'I am not really a planning person at all,' she went on. 'I don't know what I will do tomorrow and I certainly don't know where I shall be or what I shall be doing in five years.

'But age doesn't worry me. Perhaps because luckily I don't really believe I am beautiful anyway. I don't have the fear of losing my looks. Anyway, being a great beauty – or an actress if you like – is not the basis for life. There has to be more than that. The thing is to keep looking for the something else.'

In stark contrast to the opinions of those who had prophesied trouble and disruption between the two actresses, filming went smoothly, and soon the pair had been nicknamed after Mexico's two tallest mountains, which were providing the backdrop to the location – Popacatepetl and Ixtac-cihuatl. During one evening's relaxation, Brigitte revealed a hitherto unknown aspect of her acting ability – that of mime – when she appeared dressed up as Charlie Chaplin and gave a marvellously evocative performance of the Little Tramp's shuffling walk and pathetic gestures.

Louis Malle had every reason to be delighted with the result of his gamble, for when *Viva Maria!* was premiered the critics, too, were appreciative. Alexander Walker, another important London critic wrote, 'Instead of locking them in rivalry, Malle has joined them arm in arm in a duet. They don't compete for the camera, but share the honours so evenly that it is impossible to prefer one to the other.'

At the premiere, Malle expressed a cer-tain concern for Brigitte's future, saying: 'She can't go on being a French sex symbol for ever. I've been urging her to go to Holly-wood and she's seriously considering it – but she's lazy, doesn't like having to learn English. If she were American, she'd have been a sort of Marilyn Monroe, a funny, appealing idiot. But there's no scope for that in France.'

Whether the director's urgings had any-thing to do with it or not, Brigitte *did* at last cross the Atlantic to visit Hollywood and New York for the very first time in December. Her decision had obviously

Brigitte and her co-star, Jeanne Moreau, arrive in Mexico to film *Viva Maria!* in January 1965 and throw press and public alike into ecstasy!

been to a degree influenced by the fact that she owned a share of the profits of *Viva Maria!* – which was just about to open in New York – but she still had to overcome her deep-rooted fear of flying. Bob Zaguri went along to help.

Brigitte flew from Paris to New York on 16 December and Bernard Valery of the *UK Press Gazette*, who accompanied her all the way, was moved to write a little later, 'In thirty years of journalism I have never seen such a dazzling performance as that put up by this thoroughly scared girl on her first visit to the United States. She made tough American newspapermen and women eat out of her paws.'

He went on: 'Brigitte was mobbed, hit in one eye and thoroughly scared while entering the Astor theatre for the New York premiere of *Viva Maria!* She was able to enter in orderly and grand fashion the Bruin Theater for her West Coast premiere because Hollywood has a long tradition of organising such events. Hollywood natives, anyway, have seen all the greatest stars in the world and they don't get excited easily.

'What made the girl's discovery of the United States, and vice-versa, a real triumph were the three press conferences she gave. One, on 16 December on our arrival at the Kennedy Airport, one the following day at the Plaza Hotel before two hundred cameramen and reporters, and finally one on 20 December at the Los Angeles airport.'

At the New York press conference, Bernard Valery said, BB gave as good as she got. 'She fielded often absurd, sometimes insulting questions with aplomb and wit. She drew a number of genuinely appreciative laughs from people who are not easily impressed.'

One such person was the esteemed Vincent Canby of *The New York Times* who filed this report on 17 December:

'What does Brigitte Bardot really want to be?

'"Myself."

'"What is that?"

'"Look!"

'With this invitation, the thirty-one-year-old French actress, whose initials have been synonymous with sex appeal for almost a decade, began her first official visit to the United States yesterday afternoon at a twenty-minute news conference at Kennedy International Airport.

'The blonde star of *And God Created Woman* and some thirty other films brushed aside questions about her sympathies in the Vietnam war ("I did not come here to talk about politics") and concentrated instead on the kind of revelation expected of a movie queen. Asked what she meant when she once said that she would never be sixty years old, she laughed and said she expected science to find something to prevent that fate-worse-than-death. She answered most of the questions in very serviceable English.

'In a tight-fitting raspberry knit dress, Miss Bardot appeared completely at ease in the crush of more than two hundred reporters, photographers, private policemen and airport employees who pushed in on her during the interview. Asked why she had waited so long before visiting this country, where her films have probably made more money than those of any other French film personality in the last nine years. she gave a

A stunning photograph of Brigitte as the showgirl in Viva Maria!

144

plug for her newest picture, *Viva Maria!*, which she feels is one of her best and whose opening here is worthy of her attendance. Other more cynical opinion is that she may feel that her box office appeal here has been slipping and is in need of a shot in the arm.

'Following the airport formalities, the actress slipped back into her black and white striped coat and, accompanied by a ten-car motorcade, rode to the Plaza Hotel in a bubble-top limousine supplied by the Ford Motor Company. The car, once used by former President Dwight D. Eisenhower, is bullet-proof, but the only shooting yesterday was done by photographers in nearby cars. The procession slowed occasionally to allow Miss Bardot to sign autographs requested by passing motorists.

'Miss Bardot, who is travelling with an entourage of six – a hairdresser, a dress designer, a business agent, two press agents and a Brazilian friend – will remain in the United States six days.'

Interest in Brigitte was equally strong – though not so demonstrative – when she flew on to Hollywood. For the first time, the uncrowned Queen of the Screen was in residence in the Film Capital of the World. Both evidently enjoyed the other. Remarkably, although Brigitte toured the city, visited the sights and went partying with Paul Newman, Robert Mitchum and George Chakiris, it was an incident in Schwab's Drugstore which most delighted her. Bernard Valery was there to report it:

'We were showing Brigitte around one morning, driving along Sunset Boulevard, when I spotted the equally famous Schwab's Drugstore. When Hollywood was the dream factory it no longer is, stars and starlets used Schwab's as their home from home. Phone calls from agents or studios were received there, a dime was bor-

rowed, a contract was signed. Schwab's is Hollywood. We took Brigitte into Schwab's and roamed through the drugstore. She fell for a particularly attractive blue and gold container for toilet paper.

'"*C'est formidable, c'est fantastique*," she almost shouted with delight. I bought it for her: it seemed the least I could do. Whereupon Brigitte threw her arms around my neck and kissed me again and again on both cheeks. As my Fleet Street friends have taught me to say, "They call it journalism, my Lord!"'

There is little doubt that Brigitte charmed and delighted America – *The World Telegram and Sun* called her enthusiastically, 'Miss World, Miss Universe, Miss Gemini 6 and 7. She is Miss Everything' – and so she returned to France exhausted, but well satisfied. The shame of it was that she was not long after to run into one of the most scathing attacks ever directed at her – from a member of the French church.

Cheers! Brigitte drinks a toast to a most successful visit to America. Over 5000 fans beseiged the opening of *Viva Maria!* in New York

1966
The Whirlwind Countess

RENCH TELEVISION, PROUD of its most famous export's triumphant tour of America, showed an hour-long documentary about the trip in April 1966. This intimate film, which caught Brigitte both in the full glare of the public and press eye, as well as off-stage relaxing and enjoying herself, had been made by François Reichenbach, a young director who had already scored a major critical triumph with a similar film about the life of American marines.

Brigitte had been approached about the idea before she left on the journey across America to promote *Viva Maria!*, and had agreed as long as Reichenbach did not get in her way. He did not – and both the star and millions of French television viewers were delighted with the result. Reichenbach's unobtrusive camera had followed her from the moment she left Orly Airport until her weary return home. Television viewers saw her at premieres and press conferences, in her hotel writing postcards and even wandering unrecognised through Hollywood wearing jeans and a sweater.

Brigitte with third husband, Gunther Sachs, in his private jet

After the show, Reichenbach said that he had found his subject both fascinating and co-operative. 'I started shooting at ten metres,' he said, 'then seven, three, and finally in the greatest intimacy.' The resultant film certainly brought Brigitte into closer focus than virtually all her previous films, and showed her as a warm, impulsive and occasionally unsure human being, sometimes quite overwhelmed by the attention she received.

One TV critic aptly summed up this impression when he wrote that she was 'a body which plunged the American male public into a great, troubled state'. The film clearly revealed the insatiable desire people had to get near BB, and provided the audience with one of its biggest laughs when Brigitte complained to no one in particular that even her bodyguards wanted to pinch her. 'Bardot is the triumph of the body,' another critic proclaimed, pointing out that BB could work her magic clothed as well as unclothed.

For some months after the trip to America, Brigitte returned to her lotus-life and a style of existence that was becoming almost routine. When this happened to BB, it was usually followed by an explosion, and once again, events ran true to form. One evening during the summer, Brigitte and Bob Zaguri were whiling away the hours in a St. Tropez restaurant when one of

Europe's most famous playboys, Gunter Sachs, wandered in, in company with Roger Vadim. A member of an immensely wealthy and noble German family, thirty-three-year-old Sachs spent most of his life away from the non-too-taxing demands of business as an industrialist, in the playgrounds of the jet-set. A handsome, charming, well-mannered man, he attracted beautiful women effortlessly, and pursued with style and panache those few who proved hard-to-get. He was as familiar a figure in the gossip columns of the world's press as BB herself – and it was perhaps inevitable that they should meet one day.

Vadim naturally introduced his former wife to the playboy, and an instant rapport was noticeable. Within days they had become inseparable and were soon enjoying themselves all along the Riviera. Sachs was enchanted by the girl at his side: 'She was quite different from what people thought of her,' he declared 'and from what I was led to believe by the things said and written about her. She is a woman of high intelligence . . . Her decisions are based on judgement – judgement and intuition.'

Then the most extraordinary things happened in a whirlwind three weeks. Indeed, the unfortunate Bob Zaguri was hardly aware that *anything* was happening until the news broke on 13 July that the couple had got married! And not in France, but in Las Vegas of all places. Brigitte had been bowled over by Sachs' proposal of marriage on 8 July – 'I am going to marry you,' he said firmly, brooking no argument, and then swept her by car and plane to the gambling capital of America. She had barely time to draw breath, let alone complain how much she hated flying, before she was repeating her vows before Judge John Mowbray. She was now Countess Sachs!

'I was married James Bond style,' was all BB could say afterwards.

'Like a fairy story and James Bond together,' added Gunter Sachs.

'It must be a joke – I thought she had gone shopping in Paris!' gasped the bewildered Bob Zaguri.

When Brigitte returned to Paris, after a honeymoon in Tahiti and still not quite sure what had happened to her, she walked into one of the harshest attacks that had ever been directed at her. It was a castigation of her life and morals by a French priest. To Brigitte, who had always lived openly and never been hypocritical about her love-life, it came as quite a shock. The attack took the form of an open letter, 'Dear Brigitte' written by a Dominican priest, Father Marie-Dominique Bouyer, in the weekly magazine, *Vie Catholique Illustrée*. He accused Brigitte of turning love into a joke, passing from hand to hand, bed to bed, swearing faithfulness until next year and occasionally crying over animals.

'Whether you believe in Him or not, dear Brigitte,' Father Bouyer wrote, 'may God forgive you for the harm you are doing us. There are countless numbers of people who have dreamed of looking like you. Your eyes, your lips, your walk, your silhouette, your natural grace, your sincerity, your love of animals, your courage in opposing the OAS.'

Then he went on, 'In eight minutes you got married again in Las Vegas. You no longer belong to M. Vadim, nor to M. Charrier, nor to M. Zaguri: you belong to M. Sachs. In eight minutes you swear faithfulness for life. If someone else comes on the

Brigitte revelling in the wide open spaces of Scotland while filming *Two Weeks in September* in the autumn of 1966

scene tomorrow whom you do not know today, will you get married again? Will M. Sachs in turn use the words attributed to your last boyfriend, M. Zaguri, when he heard about your recent marriage – that it is all a big joke? You will say that your private life belongs to you and that it can't be helped if some people are offended by it. No. Marriage is a public act . . . There are some who can make a clear distinction between the idol of the screen and the woman who lives her life as she wishes. But there are all the others who, seeking someone to imitate in their lives, do as their idol does. You offer them a joke . . .'

Immediately the attack was published, the press beat a path to Father Bouyer who expanded briefly on his letter: 'It is not an attack on divorce as such,' he said, 'But for Miss Bardot it is a different thing. She says "I have had enough, therefore I wish to change."

'She is a very great star, and this means that she has great responsibilities and obligations. But she represents life and love in the words of M. Zaguri – as a big joke. That is not love. That is not proof of a great maturity. But it is a way of living which is being shown to all who adopt the ideas of their idol.'

Whatever Brigitte may have felt about this attack, she maintained a sensible and dignified silence. In any event, the Countess had now to prepare for a new film which was to go on location in Britain in September. The film was *A Coeur Joie* (more accurately re-titled *Two Weeks in September*) in which she was cast as a model girl who uses an assignment in London away from her French lover to play the field – first with a photographer (Mike Sarne) and then a geologist (Laurent Terzieff). Unfortunately her idyll in swinging London fol-lowed by a week in a ruined castle in Scotland ends inconclusively for all parties concerned.

The film was decidedly not one of Brigitte's best, and no doubt the after-effects of her sudden marriage, plus the rumours that all was not well between her and the Count (who with his playboy-soul did not want to be tied to film sets and schedules) contributed to a performance that received little praise from the critics. Talking about the finale of the picture, Brigitte used words that some might have thought echoed her own confusion at the time:

'The audience must decide what I do next. Perhaps I marry my lover and spend my life with the dirty dishes, tortured by memories of Scotland. Perhaps I find someone else. To marry while blindly in love is dangerous; to marry without it may be fatal.'

Perhaps, though, the most interesting thing to emerge from this film was a new piece of evidence about the Bardot legend written by her co-star, Mike Sarne, the singer-turned-actor, who is one of the few film stars to have written at length on BB from a fellow actor's point of view. He also had the advantage of an off-screen as well as on-screen fling with the lady who once again weaved her magic with consummate skill. Mike called his piece 'A Definition of Stardom' and here are two extracts.

'I was an actor and had been chosen to play the part of a photographer in the film. My picture had been shown to her in Paris and she had given her approval. For she was unquestionably The Star. All others, including Laurent Terzieff, her leading man on this occasion, were merely present to fill out the background. The director, I soon discovered, was her abject creature to

152

be dangled and tormented, teased and twirled about her slender fingers.

'For publicity – and what are movies without it? – we were driven to the airport to meet her. Her appearance affected me more strongly than I can logically understand. Like others I had grown used to her picture, I had seen most of her films without being more than an ordinary cinemagoer and had become infected with that peculiar familiarity which comes with stardom. The fan knows his idol. He has been privy to her silent thoughts. He is one with her in the cerebral lovemaking that takes place in the darkened cinema.

'On seeing her in the flesh BB is unmistakable. So many women have tried to look exactly like her that one unconsciously entertains the thought that she would turn out to look like them. I have met many stars, many beautiful women, some maybe even more beautiful than her. And yet she is Bardot. Her eyes are larger, her full mouth wider. The imitations are ridiculous. Compare it, if you will, to meeting Mickey Mouse. Not the blown-up latex dummies that waddle round Disneyland but Mickey in person. Such is the effect of meeting Bardot. Her eyes are lasers that smite you from the other side of a crowded room. No man, I repeat, no man can resist them. She seems larger than life, imbued with twice as

Co-star Mike Sarne played a photographer in *Two Weeks in September*

much vital energy as other women. Her promiscuity at once becomes understandable. For her there is no such thing as sex. There is only love. Feeling pervades her every whim. Laughter pours from her. More than any woman I have met she has the power to ridicule, to pardon, to please . . .

'Self-projection onto a strip of celluloid is not merely a question of being photographed. It helps to have the basic equipment, good looks, etc., but it is not essential. Bardot was especially favoured. To come across on screen is difficult enough. For your secret childish tricks and games, affections and foibles to be turned into commerce you must have more than an idea of what makes you look good. It becomes a science, the art of looking natural. And no, you are not yourself. Or maybe you are in a projection of yourself and you cannot step back. The image might die without you.

'The image is of a young girl with high breasts and an unlined skin. Her skin glows with sunshine. Laughter and tears hover about her eyes and mouth. She is a tramp. A tramp like Charlie Chaplin, not Marilyn Monroe. She may look like an easy lay but appearances are deceptive. She is la Bardot, an aristocrat, like Chaplin's Tramp, down on her luck, a bit sluttish at times and only when it suits her. I make her sound cold and she is not that at all. The tragedy is that women are not supposed to think. It is hard to be an image. Harder still to know what an image is.'

Interesting observations – and indeed the image of Brigitte, the playboy's girl, was to come in for close scrutiny the following year in the pages of the magazine which enshrined the views of such men about beautiful women – Hugh Hefner's *Playboy*.

1967
The Playboy's Girl

ONCE THE UNHAPPY experiences of *Two Weeks in September* were behind her, Brigitte was swept into the jet-set life of her playboy husband, 'Sachsy', as she now called him. On board his yacht, *Dracula*, they cruised the Mediterranean pleasure spots, then drove in any one of his half dozen spectacular cars to the various homes he kept in France, Germany and Switzerland. Their life became one long round of parties and rubbing shoulders with the rich and famous of Europe. It was not, though, always to Brigitte's taste.

Despite the inevitable gossip about their marriage, the couple found that they had rather more in common than many people had at first thought. Brigitte might prefer the lazy, casual life behind the high barricades of *La Madrague*, while Gunter was one for great restaurants and nightclubs and being seen around, but as he said later: 'Our communion was mental and spiritual rather than practical; we communed intellectually rather than in our activities. Our view of life, our philosophy, our ethics were the same. We were in total agreement

about the things that should or should not be done.'

On the more personal side of their marriage, Sachs was prepared to admit: 'Bardot (the name he always called her by) could be full of love and tenderness one moment. The next minute she was low-key, apathetic, useless. Then again, as rapidly, she switched to wild enthusiasms. She has tremendous resources, she can do anything she wants to do.'

As the personification of the international playboy, Gunter was naturally always being asked if he still had eyes for other women, even though he had landed one of the most desirable girls in the world? And, more to the point, as he was such an impulsive fellow, what might happen if someone new caught his attention just as Brigitte had done?

'It's what happened when I met Brigitte, of course,' he agreed 'so it could happen again. And she could meet someone too. If she did, I would have to sit down and think and work out a strategy.' Brigitte, for her part, said: 'My husband has his wealth and I have mine. We are not in love with each other's money. We are equal forces. There is no boss in our marriage. Marriage is not a jail. I permit him to do what he likes. If I did not enjoy my marriage I would not hang on. I would walk out instantly.'

The very start of the year produced a

Beauty and sensuality combined in this portrait taken in 1967

157

tragedy on their doorstep. Raoul Levy, the man who had played such an important part in Brigitte's success, committed suicide in St. Tropez on New Year's Eve. Levy had apparently travelled specially to the South of France from America to see the new year in with his current girlfriend, a fashion model named Isabelle Pons, who worked in a St. Tropez boutique owned by Gunter. However, during the course of a meal she told him their affair was over. Later, he bought a shotgun at a local shop and called at a flat where Isabelle was visiting a girlfriend.

According to reports, Levy then hammered on the door and when no one answered, shouted out, 'If you don't open the door I'll kill myself.' Seconds later there was a shot and Isabelle found him dying on the doorstep with stomach wounds. It was a sad end for a flamboyant if unstable film-maker, as *Variety* noted in their obituary of 11 January:

'Levy was perhaps the most colourful French producer since the war and the most international in outlook in a French industry still mainly geared to its own markets. He also was responsible for the advent of the sex kitten Brigitte Bardot in his first important film production *And God Created Woman* directed by Roger Vadim.

'Dead of his own wounds at forty-four, Levy leaves an estranged wife and a son of seventeen. He tried to commit suicide once before with sleeping pills but was found in time in his office by his secretary. Levy made a pile with the Bardot pix and then went bankrupt in a would-be big spectacle *The Chessboard of God* about Marco Polo, which ended up a mediocre feature.'

Shortly after this tragedy, Brigitte herself was subjected to a frightening experience. While out in St. Tropez she was suddenly recognised by a group of tourists who descended on her like a pack of wolves. With no concern for her feelings, they grabbed at her hair, pulled at her skirt and thrust cameras into her face. She was only able to escape when the owner of a local boat hustled her to safety on his small craft and rowed her out to sea. The incident had a sobering effect on Gunter. 'When I heard this story,' he said, 'I began to understand why she hated going out.'

Both of them were probably glad, then, when Brigitte's next film commitment took her to Rome in March. The journey was to make a third film with Louis Malle, this time based on three short stories by the master of horror, Edgar Allan Poe. Brigitte was cast for a second time with heart-throb Alain Delon in a tale of an army officer who is haunted by a *doppelganger* (or double) which exposes him as a cheat during a card session. BB played an alluring and mysterious young woman who is partner to his downfall. The film was released as *Histories Extraordinaires*; and as *Tales of Mystery* in the UK and *Spirits of the Dead* in America.

While Brigitte was busy at the studios, Gunter decided to try his own hand in the film business and began work on a script called *Le Pari* with an American writer, Harry Matthews. Of this project, Tony Crawley says: 'Curiously enough it was the story of a playboy seducing a cover-girl. Sachs wanted his brother-in-law Patrick Bauchau (Mijanou's husband) to play the lead and everyone guessed Bardot would be the girl. She was not so keen, having suffered mightily as a cover-girl yet again in the disastrous *A Coeur Joie*; she was more ''passionated'' with the idea, though, when Gunter said he would direct. Bondsman Harry Saltzman was rumoured to be interested in a deal, but nothing came of it and the film was never made.'

Once her filming was complete in Rome, Brigitte returned to Paris with Gunter. On 13 July, the first anniversary of their marriage, the Count threw a big party for his Countess at Maxim's – also using the event to launch the latest in his string of boutiques. A week later the social round continued in Munich when Gunter opened an art gallery; afterwards they visited Gstaad and St. Moritz, again on business.

This was followed by a little respite. The young Nicolas Charrier travelled down to St. Tropez to spend the summer holidays with his mother and stepfather. The little party was completed when Rolf, Gunter's son by his earlier marriage, also came to laze away the summer days with them beside the sparkling blue Mediterranean. 'I am perfectly content,' Brigitte murmured, 'doing nothing for months on end.' She was also apparently delighted when – said a publicity handout – little Nicolas gazed hard into her eyes and declared, 'how beautiful you are, *Mamam.*'

Soon, however, the restless Gunter was off on his travels again, while Brigitte half-heartedly leafed through the scripts of a number of films on offer to her. None of them really appealed to her, so she returned to sun-worshipping. But while she dallied away the hours, interest in her life and career continued with unabated enthusiasm. In America, the enormously popular *Playboy* magazine – Hugh Hefner's gift of unattainable women in obtainable, full-colour photogravure – was embarking on a detailed study 'The History of Sex in Cinema' by two renowned critics, Arthur Knight and Hollis Alpert. Lavishly illustrated, the series naturally devoted considerable attention to BB's contribution. It was perhaps ironical that her section

appeared immediately before the pull-out centrefold 'Playboy's Playmate of the Month' – for seven years later, on the eve of her fortieth birthday, she herself was to appear on that self-same spread, unadorned and unashamed.

In the text of their article, Knight and Alpert discussed how a changing social climate and the censorship situation had enabled Brigitte to assume the crown of 'Sex Queen' from America's own Marilyn Monroe. They wrote: 'It was hardly coincidence that Bardot's ascent came at a time when Monroe's popularity had begun to wane. Significantly, BB was allowed far more latitude than MM in disrobing, and this inhibition, which is still prevalent in Hollywood, did much to further Bardot's illustrious career. Brigitte was younger than Marilyn, too, by a good eight years, and managed to combine the naiveté of a blossoming teenager with the sensuous appeal of a young sophisticate to whom making love was as natural, and as casual, as eating.

'Roger Vadim said about the film star he helped create: "Brigitte does not act – she exists." And, indeed, there was often a surprising correlation between the parts she played and her behaviour in real life. Her eroticism on the screen was honest and earthy: she forced her viewers, and we quote Simone de Beauvoir, the French writer, "to be honest with themselves. They are obliged to recognise the crudity of their desire, the object of which is very precise: that body, those thighs, that bottom, those breasts." Brigitte was equally unhypocritical in her personal life, never attempting to hide the current object of her desire nor the pleasure she took from cohabitation with the lucky fellow. For this attitude she was often censured, even in sexually liberal

159

France: but just as often she was praised, notably by the youthful new French generation of which she was both a part and a symbol.'

After recounting the highlights of her career, Knight and Alpert went on to consider her impact on society:

'Michael Mayer noted in his *Foreign Films on American Screens* that "the high point of any Bardot picture is generally her relationship to the towel. BB may be emerging from a tub or a sunbath or a couch, but generally the towel will be loosely draped over her. There will of course be occasion for motion. The towel bends, slips, drops, droops, upends and slithers away. It's all very enticing and intellectually stimulating." That last reference of Mayer's was a sly dig at the fact that Bardot's films played in the artier cinemas and at her adoption as a pet by the French intellectuals, who saw in her frank carnality a rebellion against bourgeois moral values. Vacillating between a desire to become an actress and merely being her unfettered self, Bardot made various proclamations about her artistic intentions, but they were seldom taken seriously.

'She was taken very seriously, however, as the world's leading symbol of female nonconformity. She soon developed into what became known as a "kiss-and-tell wife", which is to say that she disdained to hide her quicksilver changing of lovers from either her husband or the public. Early in the Sixties, the BB craze showed signs of diminishing, and by mid-decade, it had all but disappeared in the United States. Although she remained popular in France, Raoul Levy, who produced many of her films, complained that "the demystification of the stars, due to too much publicity about their private lives, is ruining them at the box office. There is no longer any mystery about Bardot. The public knows too many intimate things about her life. Bardot sells newspapers and magazines, but she does not sell tickets."'

It was a cruel irony that the *Playboy* study should have closed its account of BB with a quote by the unfortunate Raoul Levy, so recently dead at his own hand. And as it happened, his words were soon to be proved wrong. As 1967 drew to a close, plans were already far advanced – with the approval of both parties concerned – to pair two of the era's most famous names of the screen – Brigitte and Sean Connery, the indefatigable James Bond.

'007 + BB = TNT!' screamed newspaper headlines on 29 November when Brigitte flew to London to fit costumes for the forthcoming film. How right they were.

Brigitte as the mysterious and alluring young woman who brings about a cheating card player's downfall in *Tales of Mystery* (1967)

160

162

1968
007 + BB = TNT!

THE IDEA OF the dynamic pairing of Brigitte and Sean Connery had been conceived by a bold young English film producer named Euan Lloyd. That it came to fruition – and in a Western, of all things – was due very much to his perseverance and tenacity. Initially, Euan wanted to star Henry Fonda and the Austrian BB-look-alike Senta Berger in *Shalako*, a story about a group of European aristocrats on a hunting party in the Wild West in the 1880s. When he failed to get the necessary finance, he had a flash of inspiration – why not Connery and Bardot? Sean had just refused to star in the next 007 film, he knew, and BB was also open to offers.

First, Lloyd put the idea to Connery. 'Bloody marvellous!' he is reported to have replied. Then he sent a copy of the script to Brigitte in St. Tropez and held his breath. Back came the word – she liked it. Next he arranged a meeting between the two stars at Deauville. They also liked each other. The following day, Brigitte spoke to the press, lightly accentuating her pigeon English, 'Oh, I 'ave nevair made a cowboy peecture. I like to try something new.'

Bardot meets Bond on the set of *Shalako*, filmed in Spain in 1968

Brigitte was, of course, delighted that she would not have to fly across the Atlantic for filming. The location was to be Almeria in Spain, already the backdrop for dozens of Westerns. The publicity drums began to beat almost immediately about the pairing of BB and 007, and in no time Euan Lloyd was expressing the greatest delight at the interest Brigitte in particular was generating. She had got the year off to a memorable start when she appeared in her own £100,000 television spectacular on New Year's Eve. Gambolling on the screen in a dazzling variety of clothes (from motorcycle gear to a girl of the future) she topped everything in one sequence by wearing nothing but a transparent tricolour, and posing in front of a wind machine while the French national anthem was being played. The segment was promptly banned by the authorities and the story made the front page of every French newspaper.

Controversy also surrounded her entry into a recording studio a week later. There, with composer Serge Gainsbourg, who had written the music for the TV spectacular, she recorded an erotic version of a song he had penned specially for her called '*Je t'aime*'. Gunter, however, strongly objected to the record and prevented its release. Later, of course, Gainsbourg was to record it again with Jane Birkin and score a worldwide hit. But all Bardot fans must bemoan the loss of the original. (BB, incidentally, was later to be paired with Jane Birkin in a highly erotic film, *Don Juan 1973*.)

Controversial she may have been, but as far as French teenage girls were concerned, Brigitte was their ideal, as a survey published the week she left for Spain revealed. Although many of her voters were only babes in arms when she appeared in *And God Created Woman*, their admiration for her was unstinted. Acknowledging this recognition, Brigitte said, 'Maybe they like me because they sense I'll never settle down, that like them I am still completely available.'

By the time the cast and crew of *Shalako* were assembled in Spain, Euan Lloyd could claim with some satisfaction that Brigitte had created 'a million dollars' worth of publicity for the film.' Nor was it to end there. She arrived in Almeria in a dazzling white Rolls-Royce (registration plate 3-WR-75) with a handsome negro chauffeur named Ibe, dressed in white, at the wheel – hotly pursued by the world's press. It was not long before she was in an expansive mood with Victor Davis of the *Daily Express*:

'In her hotel she told me: "Here I am in prison. For three months in every one and a half years, I make a film. Always I am terrified at the loss of my freedom. I cannot fling open the door and step into my garden where I can laze. The sun is my drug. I need it to live."

'She's too old for the sex kitten romping so she now calls herself "a cat character", adding: "In a strange place I am a cat, for ever prowling to find a familiar odour and a safe corner. And when I can't find it, I scratch, scratch, scratch."'

Soon, though, Brigitte was putting her nervous energy to good use in the part of Countess Irina Lazaar, who casts a more than grateful eye over our hero Sean Connery, the Shalako of the title, when he saves her and the rest of the safari party from marauding Apache Indians. She had words of appreciation for Sean, too, when she gave her only in-depth interview during the making of the picture, to Nadine Liber of the American *Life* magazine, which appeared on 27 May.

'"I can't even say how much I appreciate the moral rest it is for me not to play the lead for the first time," she said. "*Shalako* is Sean's film; he carries all the weight on his shoulders. Usually in French films I did that, with a few minor actors around me. Here the cast is so great."'

Miss Liber continues her report:

'*Shalako* is being filmed in the mountains of Spain and BB travelled there "carrying my candles, my records, my entourage" – hundreds of pink candles, thousands of phonograph records and scads of friends whom she calls "my bonbons, because we all stick together like pieces of candy". Behind this portable ambience "the pretty decor I need to go on", one senses an aggressive child likely to break what she does not understand. Once Brigitte tried to break the toy, to end her life. That was in 1960 on the Riviera estate of friends.

'Now she says: "It's better that I live like an ostrich, with my head in the sand. When I pull my head out of the sand I am so blue I cannot stand it. So I live pretty, carrying around my guitars, my candles, my records, my entourage, my books. I read a lot: *The Thousand And One Nights* right now – a beautiful love story. If by page 20 a book hasn't hooked me, I give it up. Too bad if the writer has put all the best of himself on page 21.

'"In my life it's all minute by minute. If

164

something doesn't work I have the capacity of suffering the hottest torment, then erasing it and starting anew. Maybe that's what keeps me as if I were still eighteen. I could get married fifty times, almost every time I fall in love. A movie is quite another affair, like a pregnancy, except that instead of nine months it usually lasts only three. But that's the only difference. In both cases, it's the end of all freedom. Obviously it all means I'm missing something very important, a man who could tell me to stay home. Should I meet one, I could do so. The only thing I really believe in is love. And Gunter has certainly not given me what men are supposed to give women – tenderness.''

'She says her husband has been less than enthusiastic about *Shalako*. "Gunter simply said, 'A film in Mexico? It's too far away. I'll never come there.' So the production moved to Spain. He came once and said, 'Too ugly, I'll never return.' How can I possibly go on loving an absent man? Gunter is dry, artificial, always obsessed with making an impression. He took me by storm. I was on a flying carpet – serenades

A lighthearted moment during a break from filming *Shalako*

in Venice, baccarat in Nice, marriage in Las Vegas – but when that carpet landed – bang! All he wants to do is to exhibit me to the Shah of Iran, or some important Swiss businessman. I hate it. We are never alone. So I've started again noticing that men look at me with tenderness in their eyes. Why should I go on suffering?"'

If those words sounded ominous in print, they soon became reality when Brigitte returned from Spain after the picture was finished. The Count and Countess met again in Rome in August after Gunter had completed a summer of jetting around Europe and North and South America on various business enterprises including the opening of several new boutiques. Any chance of making things up was undoubtedly ruined by the *paparazzi* who dogged the footsteps of the couple wherever they went. Gunter became so enraged on one occasion that he actually attacked one of the cameramen. Brigitte had good reason for complaining later that it was the constant attention of the press that made any relationship she formed difficult to sustain with telephoto lenses intruding at every moment.

In September Brigitte worked hard promoting the opening of *Shalako* throughout Europe. In London, the film opened to cries of delight, Cecil Wilson of the *Daily Mail* leading the hurrahs: 'You have not really lived until you have seen BB in this epic British answer to the American western, wearing an immaculate top-hatted riding habit and galloping across the Spanish mountains into Sean Connery's arms.'

Brigitte was in Germany on the eve of her thirty-fourth birthday, where she attended the premiere of *Shalako* in Hamburg. Those who knew that Gunter was in Munich at the same time thought that a reconciliation might still be possible. But they did not meet, and shortly afterwards the Count's Swiss lawyers announced that he was suing for divorce on the grounds that Brigitte had 'abused the idea of marriage and left home premeditatedly'. On being informed of this, BB replied brusquely, 'That's what he says!' Although the marriage was now clearly over, it was not until almost a year later, in July 1969, that the divorce went through.

The closing months of 1968 were spent primarily with two very different men. Brigitte had for years loved sailing, and she devoted much of October to taking a course in advanced sailing techniques from Eric Tabarly, the French yachtsman who four years earlier had sailed the Atlantic single-handed. Her days spent at Tabarly's school at St. Raphael were among the happiest of the year.

Then into her life came Patrick Gilles, a twenty-three-year-old student from St. Etienne. He appeared with BB at the Paris opening of *Shalako* and before the gossip columnists had had a chance to research his past and debate his future, the couple fled the oncoming French winter by flying to the Bahamas. There they whiled away the days in a bungalow on the suitably named Naked Island, either bathing or playing golf – Patrick's favourite sport. Little was to be heard of either of them until the following March, when Patrick would enjoy the distinction of being the first of BB's lovers to win a part in one of her films.

On the town in Paris, Brigitte with Patrick Gilles, her co-star in *Les Femmes*, who was also the first of her lovers to make a film with her

166

1969
Homo-Brigittis

THE FILM which Brigitte began working on in March 1969 turned the clock back several years to find her once more in a typical French essay in passion about a frustrated girl bored by her reserved fiancé and attracted to a promiscuous young writer. After the comedy of *Adorable Idiot*, and the variety of *Viva Maria!* and *Shalako*, the new picture, *Les Femmes* was a return to the familiar territory in which Roger Vadim had made her famous.

The movie was a joint French and Italian venture, with a script co-authored by Cecil Saint-Laurent and the director Jean Aurel. Aurel was the man who had fallen out with BB during the making of *La Bride Sur Le Cou,* but now they were suddenly the best of friends. He even agreed to Patrick Gilles playing the part of Brigitte's discarded fiancé. The role of the novelist, Jerome, went to Maurice Ronet. The fact that her lover Gilles was in the picture, naturally kept reporters and photographers on their toes. They were later to make much of the fact that like his film character he, too, was

to be discarded for someone else before the end of the year. Art publisher Michael Engels and ski-instructor Christian Kalt fell under her spell and were quickly marked down as *Homo-Brigittis.*

Biographer Tony Crawley has explained the meaning of this term much loved by BB-watchers: '*Homo-Brigittis* are usually dark-haired, medium height and young: as time went on, younger. "Anyone can be my friend . . ." Anyone over forty was marked down as RFC – Ready for Chrysanthemums (their funeral). As long as they had generous "unzipped" mouths, good teeth, and sincerity, she fell for them over and over again, amassing a total of one lover a year on average for twenty years.'

Brigitte, of course, has never made any secret of her lovers, and has often spoken freely about her views on love and romance. In this particular year of *Homo-Brigittis*, she did not disappoint her fans – delivering herself of a lengthy interview in connection with the making of *Les Femmes*, which appeared in several languages as 'Faithful in my Fashion'. Here is part of her question and answer sequence:

'In your latest film, *Les Femmes*, you fall in love with a Don Juan and yet you leave him while still in love with him. Would you do this in real life?

Brigitte: I would do exactly the same in

BB with one of the beautiful young men dubbed Homo-Brigittis, Christian Kalt

real life. I would leave with good grace, even at the very summit of our love, before love began to tarnish. This is the only victory one can have in love – knowing when to quit. It's a principle I have followed all my life.

But isn't it too painful to leave in those circumstances?

Brigitte: Yes, but that is what love is – uncomfortable and beautiful at the same time.

Oscar Wilde said that fidelity is a sentimental weakness. Do you agree?

Brigitte: It's a good phrase, but I'm not sure that I understand very well just what it means. I am always faithful. That's quite moral, I'm sure. But my own moral code puts love above duty. No one will ever persuade me that one must love just for the sake of duty.

Don't you believe that there comes a time when one must discipline one's self in order to have some kind of stability of sentiment?

Brigitte: Yes, I suppose that comes with age – and wisdom.

Do you read erotic literature?

Brigitte: Oh! I've read everything from Aretino to the Marquis de Sade. I found it very good. I hope one day our erotic films will be as good as the books.

Swedish films like, say, *I am Curious* – do they come near your idea of what erotic films should be?

Brigitte: I've not seen them, but I think it calls for considerable talent to make good erotic films. It's not enough just for the people who make them and act in them to live in a country where there are no sexual taboos and where you are allowed to portray physical love on the screen. I don't think the Swedes are necessarily good at sex films just because they take the mystery out of sex. I think sex needs a little mystery.

You don't think that love and liberty go together?

Brigitte: Liberty, yes. But depriving love of its mystery, no. These films are pornographic rather than erotic and will last only so long as there is mystery in sex. When all the taboos have been lifted they'll no longer have an appeal.

Do you think then, that there is an abuse of eroticism in the cinema?

Brigitte: It is used and abused. For a long time, no one dared. Now everybody dares and they of course go too far. But on the whole, it's for the good. Perhaps it will help to establish common sense and balance in our love problems.

Don't you feel some responsibility for having started all this with your film *And God Created Woman?*

Brigitte: I just happened to come in at the moment when these things were in the air, as it were, and people wanted to ventilate things a bit. Vadim, whom I had already known for some time, helped me with this, but it's wrong to say that he created me. Believe me, I was already there! I existed, and I existed as I had already decided to exist, that is, in a way of life I had made up my mind to follow after thinking a lot about it.

But you were brought up and educated rather strictly, in almost a puritan fashion?

Brigitte: Yes, but I decided to free myself from it.

But does nothing of this upbringing remain, no prudery, no shyness, no fear?

Brigitte: Oh! All of them remain. One never really gets rid of one's upbringing and education: one only gets over it. I don't regret any of the things that remain from my upbringing. They come in very useful.

To be a great lover, what does it take? Technique?

170

Brigitte: No, just to be very loving.'

By the time these thoughts were in print, Brigitte and Gunter Sachs had been divorced. The parting was effected in the small Swiss town of Filisur near St. Moritz on 1 July, the decree becoming absolute on 1 October. Despite some of the harsh things the couple had said about each other, they spoke with mixed feelings about the end of their three-year-marriage, which the *Daily Express* headlined as 'Brigitte's "beautiful adventure" ends in Divorce'.

'Gunter just could not stay with me,' she said, 'and I was living with the memories of my wedding and our honeymoon all the time. God knows why I married when I was so much against the idea of marriage – I thought Gunter and I would live happily for ever after.'

In *Les Femmes*, made in the spring of 1969, Brigitte revealed that at 35 she and her body were in as good a shape as ever

171

The ebullient Sachs went into the causes rather more deeply: 'I must say,' the Count told George Feifer, 'I am very happy to have been married to her. I have no hard feelings, only warm and friendly feelings towards her. But these good feelings for an old friend are not what prompts what I'll tell you now. What I'll tell you is the objective truth – which is that she was not the idol of France by any accident, but because she deserved it.

'I have heard it said that Brigitte Bardot is a dumb woman who somehow has the knack of seeming clever in interviews. The truth is the opposite: she is one of the brightest women I have known. I compare her to great creative women such as Coco Chanel. This – her extremely high intelligence – is her most unknown aspect. It shows up in her writing, which is outstanding in both style and content. In fact, she should have been a writer first and, maybe, a dancer second. Acting is only her third best choice of profession. It also shows up in her conversation, which can be brilliant when she's feeling that way, with all the crackling repartee of the French intelligentsia. But she can also sit in a corner and say nothing all evening. For she's moody with the same commitment and force as when she's active.

'Whatever she does, she does with heart and soul. She puts all of herself into her enthusiasms – for animals, for example, and for lovers. Good and bad, she lives her life to the hilt, and this is a very, very high compliment to make about any person. Brigitte Bardot is more than just a whole person, she is an exponential one. My formula for her is: BB = femmefemme.'

Gunter Sachs finally summed up his marriage and his wife with great sincerity: 'What she needed from me, probably, was more peace. Brigitte Bardot loves peace and quiet – and at that time I loved travel, friends, social life. Because despite all that journalists have written about her, she is very different from her public image. She is an introvert. Her real life is an inner one.'

Sachs' view of Brigitte was particularly apposite at this time, for she had taken to spending long periods at her farmhouse at Bazoches, filling her time looking after a large menagerie of animals. Nor was her interest restricted to just her own pets – she began to lend her name to various animal protection causes, a concern which was to be increasingly in evidence as the next few years passed. BB also broke her own rule of the past few years by making a second picture during 1969 – *L'Ours et le Poupée* (released in America in 1971 under the title *The Bear and the Doll*). The film was also a change of pace – another attempt at a light comedy situation in which she played a beautiful, flirtatious Parisian snob, used to all the comforts of life, who encounters a self-centred musician, living haphazardly in the country, and finds herself engaged in a culture struggle which ultimately – and inevitably – leads to love.

Although the film, co-starring Jean-Pierre Cassel, and directed by Michel Deville, received mixed notices, the more perceptive critics commented again on how well Brigitte could act when displaying *on* the screen the forces that tugged at her when she was *off* it – the desire to live the life of an ordinary mortal when there was no denying she was a legend. The following year was to produce a still more revealing insight into this side of her character.

BB puts the touch on Xavier Gelin – son of the famous film star, Daniel Gelin, with whom she had once acted – in *The Bear and the Doll* (1969)

172

1970
The Symbol of France

RIGITTE BEGAN 1970 – the third decade in which she had been a film star – by declaring that she had come to a turning point in her career. 'I had to give myself a shake,' she said. 'My last films have not been very successful. Then with *L'Ours et la Poupée*, things began to change.'

If this judgement might at first seem a little hasty – *Viva Maria!* and *Shalako* had hardly been box office duds – it did seem that BB wanted to spend more time considering the roles that were offered to her. For some years she had had a reputation for reading scripts very quickly and, if she liked them, making an instant decision. As a person of whirlwind emotions, she might well feel 'vibrations' on one day which would make her jump at a part, but which on later reflection – and particularly in the harsh dawn of a new studio or remote location – she would regret. But no one could accuse BB of not having done her very best to please her directors – and through them her public. Now, though, she announced: 'In future I shall pay much more attention to the scripts I choose.'

How long BB spent debating her next project we do not know, but it was not until the end of May that she emerged from *La Madrague* to begin work on *Les Novices* (*The Novices*). Filmed partly in Paris and partly on the Brittany coast, the story was certainly unlike any she had done before: playing a runaway nun who tries to become a prostitute! The film had originated from a peculiar experience the director-scriptwriter Guy Casaril had undergone. 'One day when I was in Normandy by a little creek not far from Cherbourg,' he said, 'I saw a really colourful sight. A coach, full of nuns, stopped nearby. The next moment, the whole coachload was running down to the sea and changing into black bathing costumes.'

The sight fired Casaril's imagination and he devised the plot of a novice nun who flees from her convent (by swimming away from the rest while they are taking a dip) and ends up in Paris where she is befriended by a prostitute. Untrained for anything else, the novice decides on a life of prostitution herself: but at the last minute cannot face her first client. After unavailingly trying to come to terms with life in Paris, the girl decides to return to her convent and takes her new-found friend, the prostitute, with her. The two are welcomed back like lost souls.

Cast opposite Brigitte was the excellent French comedienne Annie Giradot, who made the prostitute Mona Lisa into the archetypal tart-with-a-heart. The playing of the two actresses was also beautifully controlled and by no stretch of the imagination could the film be termed scandalous, as

Guy Casaril was quick to point out:

'It is not satirical, nor is it anti-clerical or erotic in intention,' he said. 'In most French comedies, the people are funny and the situations realistic. Here it is the people who are real and the situations imaginary. I'm more interested in producing a few smiling faces than laughter.'

BB proved once again – as she had done in *Viva Maria!* – that she would not necessarily be outclassed by a genuine actress – as the sceptics declared – nor would she fall out with the other woman. Both took to each other right from the start. 'I like her as much as an actress as I do as a person,' Brigitte declared of Annie. While Giradot enthused, 'I love looking after her, doing little things for her.' Guy Casaril himself undoubtedly contributed to the happy relationship of the two women by his working style on the picture. He explained his technique during one break from shooting:

'It does not seem as if I'm working with two famous stars. It is much more as though we are three friends who have got together to make the film. It is far better working with good actresses than bad, you can rely on them so much more. And anyway, I don't like the word direct. What one is doing, above all, is placing the actor in a situation from which he can express himself. I try to get everything to conspire to make Brigitte and Annie really want to act.'

That Casaril succeeded can be judged both by viewing the picture and by reading the almost unanimously enthusiastic reviews. It is evident, too, that Brigitte was

In *The Novices*, Brigitte plays a nun who runs away from her order and then tries to earn her living as a prostitute with – amazingly – a complete lack of success!

relaxed and enjoying the film-making – an impression underlined in an interview she gave Guylaine Guidez of *Cinemonde* in June. Guidez prefaced his interview by saying that of the many celebrities he had met 'none is a better hostess than Brigitte Bardot'. He went on, 'She fills the glasses, settles her visitors, chats merrily to put them at ease. Bardot ungracious? Certainly not! I do not know a more charming girl, less like a "star", less pretentious.'

Among the subjects tackled in his talk with BB, Guidez covered her lifestyle, the pressure of fame and the future.

GG: You have lived a long time in this little flat in the Avenue Paul Doumer. It is delightful, but I expected to find more luxury around you . . .

BB: Why? Do you think that cinema stars are obliged to surround themselves with luxury? That was alright for the great Hollywood era. The important thing is to be comfortable where one lives, in a setting which one has created to one's taste, and which is like oneself. My house in Bazoches and my villa at St. Tropez are not palaces, either.

GG: In fact, you are one of the first cinema stars not to play at being a celebrity. You have decided to give up all these 'outward signs of fame' such as jewels, palaces, sumptuous clothes, sensational parties, the best cars – though you used to have a Rolls . . .

BB: For me a Rolls is a big car in which there is room, where one can hide, travel in company, and rest. It is a utility car. I am sorry it is so expensive. Anyway, I bought it second-hand. I hate waste. I shall probably sell it.

GG: Is it also for economic reasons that you do not buy your dresses from the famous couturiers?

BB: Not at all! I think the clothes you find in the little boutiques are more attractive. But the famous couturiers have made some progress, they have begun to abandon their high and mighty ways. Now I go to Dior when I need a beautiful dress. Marc Bohan is a pal of mine. It is terrific to have a pal in that stronghold which I used to regard with some fear and which I found inaccessible.

GG: Do you like present-day fashions?

BB: They are very becoming for women. I think that girls are getting prettier. They are good at make-up. They all look rather like cover-girls.

GG: Tell me about your house at St. Tropez.

BB: *La Madrague*? I am going to sell it. You see, that house is to St. Tropez what the Arc de Triomphe is to Paris. People come to see it. There are boats which do the trip at ten francs a seat to come and see the house. Besides, one must have a change! I should quite like to have something in the Bahamas, but it is a bit far. Or in Morocco. Or perhaps no house at all! I want to travel. There are still heaps of countries that I don't know!

GG: The problem for you is surely to be able to travel without being pursued by a pack of photographers?

BB: They are incredible, the photographers! I don't know how they always manage to get to know what I am doing! I have noticed one thing: as I like to go to the same night-clubs, I suspect the waiters are in league with the photographers. As soon as I arrive, they get in touch with them. And that is the end of any peace!

GG: Do you think that this interest the press has in you will lessen one day?

BB: It is my impression that it will not happen tomorrow!

GG: So what about the future?

BB: I never think about the future. For me, the future consists of films to be made, good ones by preference to make me forget the less good.

GG: What have you down on your programme?

BB: I don't like to talk about my plans. After *Les Novices* which I am making at present with Annie Giradot, there will be *Boulevard du Rhum* directed by Robert Enrico. There's no secret about that. After that, well, I think I might be Odette Swann in *A la recherche du temps perdu* produced by Luchino Visconti. But you know, I may change my mind again!

There was no change of heart about *Boulevard du Rhum*, however, and Brigitte was kept busy on locations in Mexico and British Honduras from the middle of September until almost the end of the year. Again the film was based on fact – though this time on something rather more substantial than a crowd of nuns cavorting on a beach. Director Robert Enrico had adapted the film from a book by Jacques Percheral, a larger-than-life French adventurer whose exploits in revolutions and various nefarious activities had earned him three death sentences – from all of which, needless to say, he had escaped. The film was a thinly veiled account of some of his activities in the guise of a rum runner during the 1920s prohibition era. The highlight of this part of his life comes when he meets and falls in love with Linda Larue, the most famous female film star of the age, and begins a relentless pursuit of her.

Brigitte made a stunning movie queen with Cornelius Von Zeeling as the swashbuckling Lino Ventura. Their director Robert Enrico gushed with enthusiasm: 'Brigitte is a true professional. What other actress could slip so easily into the skin of an actress of the Gay Twenties? Lino Ventura is the same as ever. . . . The relationship of a Hollywood vamp and a forty-five-year-old buccaneer makes very good viewing. A sensational couple!' Anyone who has seen this film – sadly and inexplicably not released in either Britain or America – will surely share this verdict.

Appropriately, after playing a movie queen on film, France honoured Brigitte for being one in real life by using her as the model for a new version of the bust of Marianne, the traditional spirit of the French Republic. This anonymous spirit of the Revolution had first been sculpted in 1848, but for the new version Brigitte's figure was captured by the sculptor Aslan. Not surprisingly, it soon found a ready market. Jean-Jacques Servan-Schreiber the politician and founder of *L'Express* newspaper, to which Brigitte had taken her OAS troubles, bought one and declared: 'We should be as proud of her as we are of Roquefort cheese and Bordeaux wine. They are the products that bring us the most profit.'

Brigitte Bardot, who had once scandalised the society in which she lived, was now on view to the world as its symbol. What a transformation!

Brigitte with Jane Birkin in the erotic scene from *Don Juan* (1973) which grabbed headlines all over the world

1971-1972
The Female Don Juan

BY A STRANGE TWIST of fate almost the moment after BB had been immortalised as the spirit of Marianne, her career went into a period of doldrums and she withdrew from public view as frequently as possible. Brigitte's choice of film for her next project certainly did not help – it was another western, but lacked the originality of *Viva Maria!* or the chemistry of *Shalako*. And this was despite BB being cast opposite Claudia Cardinale – 'Italy's Brigitte Bardot' as a number of the papers had already nicknamed her.

The picture was called *Les Petroleuses*, which translates rather misleadingly into 'The Oil Girls' and was therefore retitled for international release as *The Legend of Frenchie King*. It was Guy Casaril – he of the nuns-on-the-beach inspiration – who brought the script to Brigitte. Shooting was to take place in Spain in Madrid and Burgos through the scorching hot summer of 1971. The story was set in New Mexico in the 1880s in a one-horse town named Bougival Junction where the Sarrazin family of four brothers and a sister (Claudia Cardinale) are more than delighted when a new family of five beautiful girls (led by BB) move in. What no one knows is that these are the daughters of a hanged outlaw named Frenchie King, and from time to time they dress up as men and carry out

raids to keep his legend alive. Trouble rears its ugly head when CC and BB dispute the rights to a piece of land on which oil is believed to be located. However, the interference of the sheriff (Michael J. Pollard of *Bonny and Clyde* fame) ultimately reunites the girls and drives their respective brothers and sisters into each others arms. Now doubled in strength, Frenchie King's gang ride off into the sunset.

The voracious press naturally predicted fireworks when the two leading ladies met on the set, but in fact they got on famously. Their roles, too, were different enough to allow them equal elbow room on the screen – Brigitte with the challenge of playing the very feminine Louise and (when disguised) the cruel and ruthless Frenchie King, and Claudia the matriachal figure of Maria Sarrazin. Brigitte had, of course, been a sex symbol for longer than Claudia, but the Italian girl had earned comparison with her through acting skill as well as perseverance under just the same kind of pressures that has beset Bardot. Brigitte was quite prepared to smile graciously for the cameras and declare, 'CC comes after BB, *naturellement.*' She was still undeniably Number One.

Director Christian Jacques, delighted to find two famous actresses in such accord, set about the project with enthusiasm. 'I think it is a lively and eventful story that does justice to the talents of its heroines,' he said. 'Brigitte was very brave because she hates physical pain. Claudia is a real tomboy – up in the mornings early to ride and shoot.' What he had particularly in mind when he spoke was a crucial scene in the film which called for BB and CC to fight like a pair of cats. 'I was in a cold sweat over it,' he recalled. 'It had to look authentic and I asked the two actresses not to hold back. They set to with such a will that I was afraid I'd have an invalid on my hands. But it was all right in the end, nothing worse than a few bruises.' Once seen, this remarkable fight sequence is never forgotten and makes the generally uninspired picture still worth viewing.

With no immediate plans ahead of her, Brigitte decided on a complete refurbishment of her various homes. In Paris, she made drastic changes to her apartment in the Avenue Paul Doumer, and bought a modern penthouse in the Boulevard Lannes. This she furnished starkly, although allowing herself a sumptuous canopied bed and a circular bath raised to the height of the huge picture window which gave a panoramic view of the Bois de Boulogne below. She also made extensive changes at *La Madrague* (forgetting, seemingly, her statement to Guylaine Guidez, that she was going to sell it), spending seven months removing walls, changing the size and colour schemes of several of the rooms, and importing a whole range of modern furnishings. The farmhouse at Bazoches also came in for some renovating at this time.

There were changes in her personal life as well. The former ski-instructor Christian Kalt, who had been by her side for over a year and who some were predicting would become her fourth husband, was seen leaving *La Madrague* along with the rejected furniture. Hardly had the dust settled on all this activity, than a very familiar figure walked onto the scene once again – Roger Vadim. He and Brigitte had remained friends over the intervening years since their separation and Brigitte felt in need of his counsel. In particular she wanted guidance about her future, as Willi Frischaeur has written:

'She needed her first husband, her first mentor, her most loyal friend and steadfast admirer to take her back to her beginnings,' he says 'Vadim took one long hard look at her and decided it was time for the legend of the child-woman to be buried. Since she was within sight of her fifth decade with only a couple of years' grace before crossing the threshold, he gently steered her into a position where she could still say she was thinking of men but could not yet be suspected of thinking also of – women . . .'

It was immediately evident that Vadim had a new idea for a film that would reunite him with his former wife. The partnership had produced box office dynamite before, why should it not do so again? After all, no one was more cunning and ingenious than Vadim when it came to promoting his own products. Frischauer again tells us: 'When it came to projecting Brigitte in the colouring of his own design he still had no equal. A dash of personal philosophy, a suspicion of popular sociology, were the ingredients of his new publicity cocktail . . . He was delighted when the announcement of his new film was followed by predictions that he and Brigitte "the scandalous couple of yore" together again sixteen years after *Et Dieu Créa la Femme*, were preparing another assault on their old enemy: bourgeois morality.'

The film was to be called *Don Juan 1973*. But who would play the title role? Back came Vadim's startling proposal: 'The Don Juan of our day is a woman,' he said, 'Brigitte Bardot in real life!'

Vadim, who had already revealed Brigitte in all manner of situations with men, now proposed to show her in something he had not tried before – a lesbian relationship. He knew full well that nothing was further from her inclinations in real life – but there was the screen challenge. It was one that intrigued Brigitte, too – and when had Vadim ever failed her before? So the old master worked on his script through the winter of 1971 and into 1972, calling on the additional talents of Jean Cau, the award-winning French novelist who had interviewed BB so splendidly for *L'Express* in 1962, and Jean-Pierre Petrolacci. The working title of the picture was *Don Juan 1973 ou Et si Don Juan était une femme* (released in English as *If Don Juan were a Woman*) and to star with BB, Vadim recruited two accomplished actors, Maurice Ronet and Robert Hossein, along with the British actress Jane Birkin who had made such an impact in her nude scenes for Antonioni's film *Blow Up* in 1966. It was she who was to share her bed with Brigitte, BB playing an immoral, heartless woman prepared to drive men or women to the very edges of eroticism or despair in order to gratify her own sensuality. Even a priest was not safe from her allure.

Vadim filmed his story amidst mounting speculation as to just *what* was happening on the sets. Then he spoke frankly about his intentions, in particular with regard to Brigitte.

Brigitte caught in an intimate moment with her photographer-lover, Laurent Vergez

'There is no female myth now,' he began. 'Suddenly women have lost their mystery. They're on the same level as men. *Don Juan* is the end of a period – problems about love and sex, cruelty and romanticism on an aesthetic level – and I wanted to finish that period with Brigitte because I started with her as a director. Underneath, what people call "The Bardot Myth" was something interesting, even though she was never considered the most professional actress in the world.

'For a few years, since she has been growing older and The Bardot Myth has become just a souvenir, I have wanted to work with Brigitte. I was curious about her as a woman and I had to get to the end of something with her, to get out of her and express many things I felt were in her. Brigitte always gave the impression of sexual freedom – she is a completely open and free person, without any aggression. So I gave her the part of a man – that amused me.

'What is interesting in the character of Don Juan, which has been adapted so many times, is the sense of defiance on every level. It's someone who refuses to be involved in any system. In the film it's a woman who defies men, and I do the film like the character – against all the rules. To do a movie which doesn't follow the rules is dangerous. The world is going faster every minute. To wake people up you have to hit them with a hammer, and a director has to go very far – that's the only way to talk to people today. But I thought it would be interesting not to be fashionable, it's time for aggression and violence in sex and eroticism, but I refuse to shock. I used to shock people, but today people are shocked because I don't shock. In *Don Juan* I was interested in the idea of seduction, not what happened in bed – though I would love to make a documentary on how they fucked.'

And referring to the scene in which Brigitte and Jane Birkin made love in bed, he added: 'If there's homosexuality between men they have to be queer, but women can have relationships with other women without being dykes. Brigitte seduced this girl to get at her man, and the girl is enchanted not to be treated as a sex object for once in her life.'

Reports testify that BB once again got on well with her co-star Jane Birkin. And Jane, for her part, was very happy. 'I loved working with Brigitte. She is so beautiful,' she said and also echoed BB's trust of Vadim: 'He's not a destructive director like some I've known.'

Despite their previous achievements together, there can be no denying that this Vadim-Bardot vehicle was not the artistic or commercial success they expected. The French critics were less than kind, and *Variety* was only grudgingly entertained: 'Chalk this up as a rather quaint tale of a woman finally punished for her ways by being burned alive,' wrote Gene Moskowitz. 'BB at thirty-eight still looks good but is not up to giving this the outright *femme fatale* or tongue-in-cheek quality that might have made this attempted Don Juan distaff fable more palatable.'

There were some critics who suggested that having suffered the retribution of her misdemeanours in the finale of *Don Juan 1973*, Brigitte should now leave her film career in the embers and not risk tarnishing her legend any further. But would BB take such advice?

Brigitte has suffered cruelly for her fame – yet survived to become a legend in her own lifetime. A picture from *Boulevard du Rhum*, made in 1970

ème Année N° 19   Samedi 4 Mai 1974   **75 P.**

cinés
D'ORIENT

V PROGRAMMES ☆ SPECIAL SUPPLEMENTARY PAGES IN ENG

Brigitte
Bardot

1973-1974
D'un Certain Age

I N 6 JUNE 1973, mid-way through making her next film, which had the extraordinary title *L'Histoire très bonne et très joyeuse de Colinot Trousse-Chemise* (thankfully shortened to *Colinot – The Petticoat Lifter*) Brigitte told an interviewer from French radio, 'This will be my final film. Twenty years in films is enough. I find the effort of trying to look beautiful from eight in the morning until late at night rather terrifying.'

The effect was sensational both because of the time and the place. The Movie Queen was on the verge of her fortieth birthday, and she made the announcement like some monarch of old in the magnificent Castle of La Motte Fénélon, home of the famous Bishop of Cambrai. She was wearing the most sumptuous costume for her role in the film – and on her head was a fantastic headdress created by Pierre Salnelle. A Queen of France could not have chosen a more impressive way to bid her loyal subjects farewell.

It was a statement that BB had delivered before, of course. She had threatened to retire from the screen on previous occasions, citing a variety of reasons, and then returned within the year. This time, though, fans and newspapers alike felt she might just mean it – or at the very least for a longer period than before. Beyond that traumatic age barrier of forty what would there be for her to prove?

Victor Davis of the *Daily Express*, another long-term Bardot-watcher, headlined his story of the announcement with words that mirrored the general feeling: 'Brigitte – she's no longer a kitten but she still purrs far too sexily to say "*Finis*".'

He wrote: 'So Brigitte Bardot has gazed admiringly into the mirror once too often and discovered that the sex kitten is getting to be a comfy old tabby cat. Still fairly sleek, mind you. It's still worth stroking her back. She still purrs beautifully. But she is an impetuous mademoiselle, so we must take her departure with a dash of Gallic cynicism. I mean, think of all those Jeanne Moreau, sensual middle-aged women roles she is just about to grow into. One centime will get you a hundred that she will eventually find a return irresistible.'

In *The Sunday Times*, Meriel McCooey considered the announcement from a woman's point of view and was full of admiration for how little BB had changed over the years.

'Her body,' Ms McCooey wrote, 'sug-

Brigitte's decision to quit the screen put her on the front pages of newspapers and magazines everywhere, and generally aroused the kind of comment only truly legendary figures receive

gests that she's getting out while she's still on top: her 35-23-35 statistics are exactly the same as when she started in films in 1952. Her fans have multiplied and stayed with her, and to many men of all ages she is a goddess, not one of the unattainable sort like Garbo but a sexual object who appears nevertheless to be independent and free; not just the girl most likely to, but the girl who most certainly would if it suited her.'

While the speculation went on, Brigitte got on with filming in the castle and along the Dordogne Valley. Set in France in the middle-ages, the picture was an amusing and colourful romp about the irrepressible Colinot Trousse-Chemise – so nicknamed because of his incredible success at lifting women's skirts – and his adventures across the countryside with a series of ladies including, naturally, BB whose knowledge of love teaches the philanderer (played by Francis Huster) his most important lesson: that it is easier to possess a woman's body than her heart. Few women could have played the role of Arabella with greater insight, instinct and knowledge than Brigitte: and she gave it everything, as if wishing it to be a finale of which she could be proud.

Meriel McCooey also noticed in her article how female-dominated the film production unit was and wondered if this was 'by chance rather than by design'. She continued: 'The director is Nina Companeez, who also wrote the script, the producer is Mag Bodard, and even the production manager is female. Did Bardot mind this? "Not at all," said Nina Companeez. "When she agreed to do it I was surprised. It was only ten days' work, but Bardot, who gets bored, said: "Then it will be the first film I'll be sorry to finish." Will she retire? "It gets harder for her to start new films with new directors, new crews and fresh

problems. She is a woman driven wild by life. But she is very sincere and at the moment she means it."'

Tony Crawley, who also shared the nagging doubt as to whether BB was really going to disappear from the screen for ever, pointed out that the picture was her first costumed role – although she had, of course, appeared in sketches such as that in *Les Amours Célèbres* and *Histoires Extraordinaires*. He further noted that Arabella – even though she was a medieval courtesan – was 'remarkably close to the omnipresent BB image: seducing, never seduced, living with her own hand-picked retinue of lovers and other hangers-on'. And he added 'Her *chevalier*-servant in the group was her own latest lover, since *Don Juan 1973*, Laurent Vergez – her second lover, incidentally, to appear in two films with her.'

The film is an absolute delight, with Brigitte displaying her range as an actress from the moments of high drama to skittish comedy – as well, of course, as her own delectable body, 'still in stately shape' as *Variety* noticed in its review. For all these reasons *Colinot* deserves a place in any half dozen of BB's best films.

Brigitte slipped into her retirement with a round of interviews, declaring philosophically, to one journalist, 'I'm retiring because if I don't abandon films they may abandon me.' While she consoled another with that famous smile of hers 'No need to panic. What is more beautiful than an old lady with white hair grown wise with age and able to tell lovely stories about her past?' These turned out to be much more prophetic words than anyone – even Brigitte – realised at the time, for she later decided to film her life story.

A year of lazy abandonment to the simple life followed – no one has ever perfected the art of being happy doing so little as BB – and this took her through to her fortieth birthday. Only one moment of sadness blurred this idyllic period: the death in Paris on 3 November 1973 of Marc Allegret, the man who had first spotted her potential, although he had left it to his young protégé, Roger Vadim, to fulfill. He was seventy-three. Although Allegret's death had been of natural causes, unlike the suicide of Raoul Levy, the passing of another of the important figures in her career deeply saddened Brigitte.

For her fortieth birthday in September 1974, Brigitte assembled a group of her friends in St. Tropez and surprised everyone by holding a superb beach party at which she gave an exhibition of barefoot dancing and also sang a number of songs accompanying herself on a guitar. At a more private party at the 55 Club she blew out forty candles on a huge cake as twenty-five friends sang a resounding 'Happy Birthday'.

A scene taken from *The Petticoat Lifter* (1973), when Brigitte announced her retirement from the screen. As one of the undoubted queens of the cinema, she picked a suitably regal setting and outfit for this moment.

Among this group of friends was Françoise Sagan, the *enfant terrible* of French literature since the 1950s, who had had as big an impact on the world of letters as Brigitte on the world of films. Françoise was two years younger than her friend, but had been born into the same kind of bourgeois Parisian background and broken from it with a vivid and enormously successful testament of youthful rebellion in the form of her novel *Bonjour Tristesse* published in 1954. Like Brigitte, Françoise had suffered in her personal life – she'd had two broken marriages – and attracted the kind of sensational headlines that only the French press could generate. Though shy and rather introverted, Françoise had nonetheless formed a friendship with the outgoing and naturally aggressive Brigitte which had stood the test of time.

Françoise took advantage of her friend's birthday to begin a series of tape-recorded conversations with Brigitte about her life and career. From these emerged some interesting insights which she later published in a magazine essay, 'As We Get Older'. She began by asking what BB had done with her life.

BB: I'm a woman who's undoubtedly made a success of her career, but certainly not of her private life. Let's say someone who is incomplete. And that's why I no longer want to work. I want to try to make a success of my real life. Up to now, it's been nothing but bits and pieces.

FC: Because of your career?

BB: Films take up your time, your strength. They annihilate and imprison you. I've failed in my real life.

FS: Don't you think that, apart from your career, the fact that you're famous,

independent and rich complicates things?

BB: Certainly. It complicates your love life because the men you meet are in an inferior position – unless perhaps you meet someone who's both rich and well known. Only I don't like rich people or their sort of mentality. They think they can buy everything – including me. So if the man in my life is, let's say, an ordinary man who's not famous, then the relationship between us is immediately a false one. The couple we form is fragile, unbalanced . . .

The novelist next asked Brigitte about her family and her relationship with them.

BB: I love them, they love me. But we have never asked nor given much to one another. My family has never been a rock in my life.

FS: How did they take your success?

BB: They didn't want me to get into this profession. Later they were slightly proud in spite of themselves. And then when I led my life as I did – divorces, lovers, everything the papers wrote or invented – that really shocked them.

FS: If you hadn't gone into films, what other profession would have tempted you?

BB: I don't know, but I'm sure I'd have succeeded. I've done things besides movies and when I do them, I do them well. Look, I started singing. I'm not saying that I'm a marvellous singer but I'm not terrible. If I do fashion photos, they're pretty fashion photos. I like work that's well done.

After discussing Brigitte's childhood, Sagan asked if God or religion had been important to her.

BB: I don't know. I was raised by nuns. I made my first communion. My first marriage was in a church. But I didn't believe in the Good Lord – this nice grandfather with a white beard – for very long. On the other hand it seems to me that the world must have a creator or a guiding principle. One can't explain everything by chance. In any case there's one thing I do feel deeply: there are two opposing forces in the world, the good and the bad, which fight against each other. And I think that's also true for each of us.

FS: You have a Russian vision of existence – the good and the bad . . .

BB: Yes, there's a duel between the good and the bad. I'm afraid of war and of all violence. But I sometimes wonder if war isn't a basic need, a kind of way of getting rid of pressures.

The next topic for the two friends was Death. What were Brigitte's thoughts on it?

BB: I'm not afraid of death itself – one loses consciousness and goes to sleep. What is awful for me is that my body doesn't disintegrate when I die and that afterwards comes the resting place, embalming, smelling bad, burial . . .

FS: And the idea of making dandelions grow doesn't amuse you?

BB: Not at all.

FS: What effect does it have on you when you receive mail saying, 'I desire you'? Is it funny, irritating, depressing or exciting?

BB: Nothing, nothing at all. Those letters are completely beyond me. I look at them and throw them away.

FS: Usually people look at us as objects. It's irritating.

BB: The only important judgement comes from those who know you.

FS: Do you have lots of friends?

BB: No, I have a lot of acquaintances but few real friends. With them I don't have to play a game. I've had the same friends for twenty years.

FS: Are you tyrannical with your friends?

BB: No, I want them to be free. Of course, if they drop me or seem indifferent, I'm hurt. If I'm possessive sometimes it is from fear rather than solitude.

The conversation went on to cover the familiar topics of love and film-making which Brigitte had already enlarged upon in a hundred earlier interviews. Then Sagan asked if she had any regrets.

BB: Hundreds. You can't know how much I would have liked Picasso to have done my portrait. Perhaps because it's something I could have kept. I met Picasso at the Cannes Film Festival when I was eighteen. I wasn't well-known – I was nothing at all. Well, he invited me to his house. He was adorable. He told me many things and then I never saw him again.

FS: Are you fascinated by famous people? For example, Napoleon, Mae West, Joan of Arc?

BB: No, such people don't fascinate me. I reserve my admiration for someone close to me who does something ordinary but difficult for him to do, or for someone who is dedicated to something, like a nurse.

FS: Have you ever dreamt of a handsome man, like Burton, for example? Do you dream of Burton?

BB: Do I dream of Burton? No!

FS: Do you have a sense of humour?

BB: Not enough.

FS: Oh yes, you have. It's a precious thing, isn't it?

BB: Let's say I'm good at repartee when everything's going well. But if things are going badly, if I feel desperate, then I completely lose my sense of humour.

Predictably, Sagan ended the conversation by asking Bardot what the future held for her.

BB: The myth of Bardot is finished. But Brigitte is me. Perhaps in five years people will have forgotten me, perhaps not. I'll be forty-five. I won't be too much the worse for wear. And I'll finally be able to live like everyone else. I'm waiting for that moment, I dream about it. I'll do the things I like, and I alone will be responsible. I'll no longer be a beautiful object but a human being.

Of course, the myth of Bardot wasn't over then, and still isn't over today. Events were already conspiring to keep her image before the public eye, albeit in another medium. To mark her birthday, Brigitte had allowed her boyfriend Laurent Vergez to take a stunning series of nude photographs which were published in the American magazine *Playboy*. 'Bardot in her fortieth birthday suit' was one comment – and there was no denying she carried her age as well as a woman ten or more years her junior. And those pictures were also to herald her appearance in a spectacular advertising campaign.

Brigitte still playing nude scenes with great style in her last film, *The Petticoat Lifter*

192

1975-1976
The Fragrance of Success

BRIGITTE HAD, OF course, begun her career as a model, and apart from fashion poses she had also appeared in a number of advertisements during those early years – including a delightful series for Lux soap. So it was perhaps not too much of a surprise when she allowed herself to be lured from retirement to star in a television commercial.

In the years since those early advertisements, BB had registered her initials as a trademark and they had provided another lucrative source of income for her, along with the use of *La Madrague* as the symbol on a range of clothes. She herself, though, had turned down offers to promote items in person. But this rule had been broken once, in 1974, when the French Tourist Authority appealed to her to help promote her native land. Always a patriot (she had pointedly refused to change her citizenship when she married Gunter Sachs), this was an invitation she felt duty bound to accept. As one of *la belle France's* most famous products, she was required to help sell its attractions to potential visitors – Americans, in particular.

The thirty-second commercial was made partly in studios in Paris and partly on location, and she made a most appealing and persuasive saleswoman for the gastronomic pleasures of France – its cheeses, wines and pâtisseries – as well as its scenic delights: the beauty of the Dordogne, the castles of the Rhône valley, the mountains of the Haute Savoie and, naturally, the beaches of the Riviera. Extolling the delights of the country in her most seductive tones, she added as a punchline, 'After all, I am still a child of France . . .'

The advertisement was attractive to the eye in more ways than one, and it inspired the executives of Goya Perfumes to believe that she was just the person they needed to sell their new men's toiletry *Zendiq*. But how to get her to do it when she was turning down all the scripts and projects which still flooded in? It took a year of negotiating to convince Brigitte and her long-time agent, Olga Horstig Primuz, who has handled her interests from the outset of her career, that it was a worthwhile project. Michael Pitt-Bailey was the man at Goya who had the determination and the patience to set up this deal and create a piece of television history. He said at the time, 'We decided that we would like a woman to project *Zendiq* for us. For us there was only *one* woman, and that was Bardot.'

To begin with the company had to

Time now to relax and enjoy herself – Brigitte in 'retirement'

195

explain all about the product to Brigitte. First, the name. *Zendiq*, they said, was a word used by ancient civilisations to describe men who were ostracised for their strong beliefs – so the *Zendiq* man was a person who was a law unto himself. He was envied for his strength, his charisma and his individuality. Secondly, the constituents of the products. These were the fragrances of oils of Vetyvert, Iris Absolute and Sicilian Lemon, blended with Tobacco, Chypre, Patchouli, Sandalwood and various Oriental spices. Thirdly – when Brigitte had agreed in principle to the deal – she helped choose the final blending of these ingredients, approved the smell, as well as the bottle and packing. Even the embossed silver medallion which represented an ancient symbol for the spirit of life had to get her okay.

This eye for detail proved to the Goya executives that they were dealing with a very shrewd businesswoman. Her fee was agreed at £100,000, which along with the production costs (the film set was an exact reproduction of Brigitte's sitting room in *La Madrague*) put the total cost at around half a million pounds. Several of Brigitte's earliest films had cost less than this added together.

Even the fee and satisfying Brigitte as to the quality of the product still did not entirely explain *why* the solitude-seeking actress had made the commercial. Meriel McCooey in a special feature in *The Sunday Times* Colour Supplement entitled 'And A Commercial Was Created' thought she had the answer: 'Precisely how it was done is not stated. Goya does not claim that it sprinkled its representatives with *Zendiq* before despatching them to the negotiations. However, one Goya employee declares that "if you mention anything about wild life preservation she almost eats out of your hand", a valuable piece of information to any man who would like to have Miss Bardot almost eating out of his hand.'

The remark about BB's involvement with animals was a reference to what was taking up some of her time since her withdrawal from the film world and it is a factor we shall return to shortly. Some of the techniques she learned from advertising she was also to employ in her campaigning for animal rights.

Filming the commercial took just one day, and the smoothness was no doubt due to the fact that two of the most important members of the crew had already worked with her before: director Michel Deville on *L'Ours et La Poupée*, and cameraman Claude Lecomte on *Les Novices*. Brigitte also brought her own make-up man and hairdresser and a selection of her own clothes. She worked for twelve hours non-stop and left Michael Pitt-Bailey full of praise.

'We started by using a man with her, but honestly he was quite superfluous,' said Pitt-Bailey later. 'We played music and because she knew almost everyone and felt she was among friends, she loosened up and was soon dancing barefoot around the studio. She loves dancing and moves quite beautifully. Maurice Pascall, my associate, and I watched the rushes of course, and we saw the film the first day after shooting, but we really didn't know what we had, we could not be objective about it. We ran the film for store buyers and chemists at six or seven receptions, but it wasn't until we showed the finished product to the women's press and some gossip columnists – who clapped, who *actually* clapped – that we were aware we did have something really special on our hands.'

196

Meriel McCooey herself was convinced that when the commercial was shown it would attract 'to the accompaniment of heavy breathing throughout the land, an audience larger than *Coronation Street*'. The London *Evening Standard* which decided to monitor the impact for itself, proved her right. The advertisement was first shown on the evening of 4 November (so as not to clash with the fireworks of 5 November Guy Fawkes Night) and referring to the event as 'some kind of milestone in media history', reporter Mary Kenny said, 'Last night people were actually telephoning the commercial television companies and asking what time the BB ad. was coming on.'

Miss Kenny went on: 'It appeared, as many millions will have noticed, as the second advert after the 10.15 commercial break on ITN's News at Ten. Just after a down-to-earth Government exhortation to save water she appeared, swathed in hats and chiffon and a blue cloud, saying in musky Franglais, "I know my man and he wears *Zindiq*", and then she was gone, like all sudden visions, in a trice.'

Mary Kenny sought the opinions of a number of viewers, including Mary Parkinson, wife of TV chat show personality Michael Parkinson, a self-confessed Bardot fan. 'It certainly made me curious,' said Mrs Parkinson, 'If I saw the product in a shop tomorrow, I'd have to go and smell it, and I'd accept a sample, but the advert alone wouldn't make me buy it straight off. It was very beautiful in an unreal way, you thought – she's so perfect and, of course, she's forty, but she's not an ordinary forty – she's just not real. I think the advert would appeal to women, but in a fantasy sense. I am sure Michael would have preferred to see her in black suspenders.'

Was the commercial a success? Mary Kenny pointed out that it is women who buy the bulk of men's toiletries, and that the advertisers' thinking was that as BB was the woman other women wanted to look like, by buying *Zendiq* they became like her. 'But,' she said, 'there is one flaw in the Bardot image for many women. Knowing a man is easy. It's holding on to them that's the difficult bit. Bardot is famous for her allure: not for her consistency.'

It was my impression that men as a whole loved the commercial, and still fancied the screen goddess that was BB. And the same proved the case when it was shown in Germany, Austria, Belgium, Scandinavia, Finland and Switzerland. Strangely, there were no showings in either France (for contractual reasons) or America. ('The white man's grave for foreign toiletries,' said Goya.)

The famous Bardot magic was, however, also at work in real life. A new lover was now sharing her time, a Czech sculptor named Miroslav Brosek, aged thirty-three, whom she had met on the ski-slopes at Meribel. He was also an actor and had appeared in films under the alias Jean Blaise. They met when Brigitte went to see a new collection of his sculptures at his studio. 'She looked into my eyes in a way that said more than words,' Miroslav said later. 'At once we were in love.'

The couple were soon being seen together at Meribel and later in St. Tropez, where Brigitte declared that her lover was helping her find the peace she so desperately needed after her hectic life. 'With Mercu (his nickname) I have become deeper, more still,' she said. 'He gives me his passion for sculpture. I give him my passion for animals. In the evenings he works. He is fantastically talented. Now I just adore to be like his wife. I am available.

197

I stay. If he needs me I am there. We are very secret and savage.'

Friends saw a greater contentment in Brigitte than they could remember for years, and only one sad event interrupted this new period of happiness. The death of her father, Louis Bardot – 'Pilou' as he had been nicknamed. His health had been steadily declining in recent years, and Brigitte visited him several times in a Paris Hospital. Although there was clearly no hope of recovery, she was grief-stricken when he did die, aged seventy-nine. Though she had rebelled against much that he had stood for, she had loved and respected him. He had clung as tenaciously to his belieefs – right or wrong – as she had done to hers. For a person who some claimed was a perpetual child, there could be no denying the impact on her of the loss of someone as important as her father.

In previous years, such a death might have had far-reaching effects on BB's personality. There might well have been a period of great depression with the usual attendant explosions. Instead, however, she channelled her thoughts on death into a new and positive phase in her life. Because of her love of animals, she had of late become increasingly concerned over the slaughter of certain species. Now she resolved to use her fame and all her powers of persuasion in campaigning against these abuses.

1977
'Madonna of the Strays'

B's LOVE OF animals has been one of the most enduring passions of her life – pursued with greater involvement and enthusiasm than her career as an actress or even her reputation as a screen goddess. Animals, any animals, cats, dogs, horses, donkeys, goats, birds, be they pets or wild, cared-for or neglected, have engaged her attention wherever she has gone. Stories about her adopting strays on location are legion, just as are the accounts of the multitude of animals she has given happy and secure homes to on her farm in the French countryside or at *La Madrague*. It is one of the most delightful traits of this beautiful woman and in part explains why she is so often compared to animals – from a sexy kitten to a naughty young foal.

As Tony Crawley has well put it: 'Ambition has never been Bardot's strongest point. The career came to her, not vice-versa. And she forever claims she never cared for the fame thrust upon her. The only occasions she has enjoyed being Bardot – or "someone" as she puts it – was in 1961 when she proved she was indeed

someone by saying *non* to the pimps of the OAS; and later when her well-chronicled love for animals led her to expose the savagery of the French *abattoirs*. She campaigned for changes in the law about the slaughter of animals. A special stun-pistol is used today instead of a club or hammer and in France the changes are known as the BB law.'

Also writing on this aspect of her life, biographer Willi Frischauer has said: 'We must never overlook the animals. Animals not only in the apartment nor just at Bazoches. When she heard that two score or more dogs were condemned to be destroyed at an animal home, she jumped into her Rolls, drove to the home and spent hours choosing fifteen animals worthy of salvation. She took them with her to Bazoches and started thinking up names for them beginning with one she christened *Betterave* (Beetroot). It was not long before Brigitte was labelled "Madonna of the Strays".'

Frischauer also recounts the story of the occasion when Brigitte became most concerned that all her animals should have a happy sex life. Mauricette Marcey, her housekeeper on the farm at Bazoches, said that her mistress once told her, 'Our hens seem bored. They need a cock!' Then she set off to the nearest market and bought the biggest and proudest cock she could find.

Brigitte the animal lover. Since childhood she has been devoted to animals, both domestic and wild, and has adopted many strays while on location

201

Brigitte showed from quite early on in her life that she would not be intimidated by anyone – whatever their position – when it came to defending animals. And this resolve had no doubt been hardened by an incident at Bazoches when a local official had cold-bloodedly set about killing some of the stray dogs she had adopted and allowed the freedom of her lands. Pieces of poisoned meat were left about at strategic spots, allegedly to 'protect the wildlife from ferocious dogs'. None of the animals were, in fact, dangerous but eight died as a result of this premeditated campaign. 'I spent whole weekends in the forest calling for my dogs,' Brigitte reported angrily, explaining how she found out what had been going on. And she added, 'The cruelty of human beings revolts me.'

BB's family of animals has, of course, constantly changed, increasing mostly. Among her favourites have been four magnificent red setters, *Nini*, *Mouche*, *Mienne* and *Macho*, an engaging little tortoise-shell cat named *Belote*, and perhaps the most irresistible of her strays, a mongrel dog called *Pichnou*.

Although she had always been ready to rush to the defence of animals through the press or in public, it was not until May 1976 that she tried to formalise this interest by creating the Brigitte Bardot Wildlife Foundation dedicated to protecting animals and wildlife. This idea had been sparked off by pictures she had seen on television of the 'culling' of baby seals in Newfoundland where men with clubs slaughtered the tiny creatures, ostensibly as part of a weeding out or selection process. The butchery of these *bébés phoques* horrified Brigitte, and she mounted a campaign of letters, telephone calls and direct approaches to politicians and other state officials to put a stop

to the cruelty. In the April of that same year she helped make an hour-long documentary film for French television about the culling, which so galvanised public interest and impressed the producers that they offered her a series on animal topics.

Instead, though, Brigitte made plans to fly to Newfoundland where the year's cull was due to take place, and there confront the hunters, defying them to continue in the face of her opposition, and by proxy that of the rest of the civilised world. However, these plans fell through, and instead BB took part in a public demonstration in front of the Norwegian Embassy in Paris. It was as a direct result of the support which she gathered for this protest that she decided to set up the Foundation which bore her name. To help her she recruited environmentalist Philippe Cottereau, polar explorer Paul-Emile Victor, and the far-famed underwater diver Commander Jacques Cousteau. And at a press conference to launch the Foundation and explain its ideals, BB was so overcome by emotion that she could do little more than stutter through tear-stained lips, 'Merci, merci'.

The work of the group got off to a good start: Brigitte delivered a memorable statement in which she declared, 'The planet is in a state of war and unless there is action by its inhabitants, irreversible accidents will put the survival of the species at risk'. But it was quickly doomed by internal problems. Four months later, in September 1976, BB declared that the Foundation was to be closed. All the plans to run a crusade against the ill-treatment of wild or domestic animals, to promote ecological research, to picket the sales of animal furs, and a determined endeavour to prevent scientific experiments using live animals, came to nothing.

The announcement attracted worldwide attention as one would expect. In a report on 20 September headlined, 'Wildlife proves too much for BB', *The Guardian* said: 'Brigitte Bardot has disbanded her Wildlife Foundation after only three months. Since she passed her fortieth birthday Brigitte Bardot has spent her time defending the interests of animals. But she has also found it difficult to fulfill the demands of those who wanted to help her. Spokesmen at the Foundation say she has been overwhelmed by the public response to her campaign and she has been flooded with letters and cheques. But she felt that there were so many problems raised that she would have had to spend all the funds on bureaucrats. "The complexity and multiplicity of problems concerning the defence of animals and the abundant show of generosity by French people who have responded to my cry of alarm have meant paradoxically that the Brigitte Bardot Foundation ceases to exist," she wrote in a letter to supporters.'

There were a number of angry recriminations between those involved in the Foundation following its sudden closure – but it had scored one major success in getting French furriers to sign an agreement renouncing the use of the skins of baby seals and other endangered animals. Brigitte later added to her personal statement by telling *The Sunday Times:* 'I certainly do love animals and I was ready to sacrifice part of my life to them. That is why I set up the Brigitte Bardot Foundation and attended all their meetings. I considered some of the

Brigitte with some of the strays she befriended while filming *Viva Maria. Following page:* Brigitte appears on television with Franz Webber to protest over seal culling

financial accounts doubtful and I therefore dissolved the partnership which I had a perfect right to do.'

In finalising the closure, BB's lawyer Gilles Dreyfus, said with a nice turn of phrase: 'Miss Bardot fulfilled her obligations, but she obviously could not be expected to spend twenty-four hours a day working for the Foundation. That is not her job. As a beautiful woman she is not prepared to enter the Holy Order of Animals.'

Despite this set-back, Brigitte did not stop her efforts on behalf of animals. She made plans to lobby official bodies about cruelty to animals, vivisection and particularly seal culling. She also made new plans to fly to Newfoundland as she had originally intended. Early in 1977 she wrote to Franz Webber, the well-known Swiss ecologist, and journalist, offering her help in his campaign against the slaughter of the seals. Webber came to Paris where they met, planned tactics and wrote letters to many world leaders including President Giscard d'Estaing of France and American President, Jimmy Carter. The ecologist was captivated by BB's energy and enthusiasm.

'I didn't know her before when "everybody" did,' he said, 'but I can tell you she is nothing like her image as a film star. She told me she has two lives in her. One was the life of the celebrity, who liked to display herself. The other – which has come to the surface now, and is the only one that matters – cares for the animal world. She is utterly sincere and compassionate. She is anything but frivolous. With her entire heart and soul she is dedicated to saving these poor baby creatures.

'Miss Bardot is generous, hospitable, and extremely intelligent. She almost dashed off her letters to the two Presidents, yet they were the work of an expert writer. She has the kind of head on her shoulders that cannot only count, but also reason and analyse. I myself am considered a person of energy and enthusiasm, but she makes sparks fly. She perceives things so quickly, is so full of suggestions and action, that everyone around her picks up some of her four-wheel drive. Once she's decided to start towards something, she jams the accelerator to the floor.'

In April 1977, Brigitte fulfilled her earlier promise to go to Newfoundland, and accompanied by Franz Webber and Miroslav Brozek, she joined in with the International Fund for Animal Welfare party which staged an actual protest demonstration on the ice-floes while the culling was taking place. Brigitte was clearly horrified at the thought of seeing the *bébés phoques* clubbed to death, but stuck to her ground, declaring, 'At the present rate of killings the last of the seals will be finished by 1985.' She also demanded that the Canadian government take action because now 'the whole world has risen up against the seal hunt'.

Although unable to stop this particular cull, Brigitte returned to Paris feeling that her mission had helped, through the vast publicity it engendered, to bring the butchery into still keener focus. She also brought with her a baby seal which she nicknamed *Chou-chou* and which happily joined the rest of her menagerie at *La Madrague*.

Franz Webber was quick to praise her actions when he, too, returned to Paris. 'Since she dislikes long travel and fears flying, going to Canada with me was an act of courage for her,' he said. 'We reached the tundra in a small plane. The ice and the blood of the seals frightened her badly. And it *was* dangerous: she had one nasty slip.

She couldn't have faced ice, helicopters and the press conference – because her very greatest fear may be of journalists – without great determination to fight to the end. Brigitte Bardot is wonderfully steadfast. She is wonderful in general – a fantastic, complete person.'

Although some sections of the press – sceptical as ever – thought Brigitte had turned her trip to Newfoundland into a kind of publicity stunt (was she thinking of making a comeback to the screen, one or two wondered?) the overall impact it created was very good. Her name had drawn attention to the plight of the baby seals, and was thereafter quoted with some impact in many discussions on the matter. One august body that thought her efforts had been most praise-worthy was the Council of Europe which invited her to attend a debate on seal hunting on 24 January 1978: the first time such an invitation had been extended to a private individual as opposed to a politician or statesman. She went gladly and was heartily welcomed by the Council President, Professor Karl Czernetz, who said, 'I believe it is not out of place for a parliamentary assembly to salute someone who, like Madame Brigitte Bardot, interests herself in the protection of seals against cruelty.' Other ordinary members of the Council paid tribute to her saying that it was largely as a result of her activities that public anger had been aroused about the 'massacre of baby seals in the Atlantic'.

The Council members agreed that although there was much still to be done in the battle against the seal cull, steps in the right direction were already being taken. Many countries were now seriously thinking of banning the importing of baby seal skins across their borders, and some –

including Holland – had already done so. From her seat in the public gallery, Brigitte allowed herself a rare smile of genuine satisfaction at work well done. Something worthwhile she really wanted to achieve was happening. Unfortunately, in the now so-familiar pattern of her life, another unhappiness awaited her just a few months away.

205

1978-1979
The Secret Life of Nicolas

FOLLOWING HER PERIOD of intensive campaigning on behalf of animals during the previous two years, Brigitte now enjoyed a time of peace and tranquillity, alternating between Meribel and St. Tropez. At the ski resort, Brigitte celebrated her third anniversary with Miroslav. The sculptor had frequently put his own desire to get on with his work second to accompanying Brigitte on her missions of mercy. She was quick to acknowledge his help in what was a tough, uphill struggle against both public indifference and powerful commercial interests.

'His loyalty has sustained me,' she said, adding that she thought her presence had in turn helped inspire Miroslav in his sculpting. Of their relationship she said, 'I believe I have at last found profound stability.' Close friends were glad to agree that the couple had now been together far longer, and seemed much happier, than in most of BB's previous relationships.

In St. Tropez, Brigitte once again demonstrated her ability as a campaigner when she took on local authority plans to build a huge new complex on the outskirts of the resort. The scheme was for the construction of an office block complete with 460 flats, and there could be no disputing that it would transform the face of the community. Although the plans had been care-fully and thoroughly presented by a leading French architect, Brigitte rode into battle along with the other protestors. She was uncompromising in her view that this scheme would result in the 'implantation of a cancer city' on the beautiful resort. She emerged from *La Madrague* looking as stunning as ever to take part in a rally attended by many hundreds of people which assembled before the Mayor's offices. She carried a banner, 'Save St. Tropez From Disfigurement' and, not surprisingly, attracted a host of reporters and photographers. The following day she was once more splashed across the front pages of French newspapers.

To the rallying call against the plan, Brigitte added her own unique impact. If the building took place, she said, she would personally quit this lovely spot which had for so long given her 'protection, charm and freedom'. Although authority never likes bowing to personal pressures such as this, the officials of St. Tropez were only too well aware of the fact that Brigitte's residence in the resort was one of the main tourist attractions. Would people no longer come if she left?

There could be only one winner. The plans were shelved and BB stayed.

The summer of 1978 came and went in the now familiar pattern of lazy, sun-filled days – only to be rudely shattered early in

September when Brigitte was informed that her mother had died suddenly in her Paris apartment. The death of Mme Anne-Marie Bardot stunned Brigitte, just as her father's two years previously had done. For the girl who was forever child-woman – according to one popular viewpoint – the last link with childhood had finally been severed.

Mother and daughter had, of course, had their ups and downs; more than most. But with her artistic leanings, sublimated though they were much of the time, Mme Bardot had still taken pleasure from her daughter's achievements. Some of the scandals had undoubtedly hurt her, and BB's sexual reputation had been a constant source of embarrassment. Yet mother and daughter genuinely loved one another and respected each other's point of view.

The anguish was clearly evident in Brigitte's face when she travelled to Paris for the funeral on 10 September. The small family gathering for this sad event also produced a surprise. Among the mourners was Brigitte's son, Nicolas Charrier, now a strapping, dark, curly-haired eighteen-year-old. Nicolas was one of the few subjects which Brigitte emphatically refused to discuss when pressed by journalists. She was anxious to protect him from the limelight that constantly bathed her. Comments by BB about her son are, therefore, few and far between.

The previous year, 1977, in a rare moment of relaxation from her rule, she told the English journalist George Feifer, 'I am very proud of Nicolas.' She went on: 'When he was born I was a star and had no time for babies. My mother took care of him for a while. If it had been a girl, it could have stayed with *Mamam*. But a boy, *non*. Much better for him to go with his father

and become a real man. He adores Mercu now and understands all the problems I had with his father.' And BB also joked to Feifer: 'My son said to me last week, "Now, mother, no more boyfriends!"'

A year on, at the time of the funeral, the *Sunday Express* pieced together the scant facts about Nicolas' life to give a picture, albeit incomplete, of what had happened in the intervening years to the infant whose arrival had been heralded as 'the most famous baby in France', and who had since been very rarely seen. The newspaper reported: 'Shortly after the baby boy was born, his parents' marriage broke up. In the aftermath Brigitte agreed that he should be brought up by his father, saying: "I am not adult enough to take care of the child. I need somebody to take care of me."

'Just what kind of childhood did Nicolas have? In the circumstances it was reasonably stable. He was cared for by nurses under the eye of both sets of his grandparents, he was educated at an expensive private school and although his mother clearly did not take a day-to-day interest in him, he did not lack for money. Holidays were occasionally spent with his mother, usually at her St. Tropez villa. And when his father remarried into a wealthy banking family Nicolas was well cared for by his stepmother.' But, said the *Sunday Express*, when that marriage broke up, young Nicolas was taken in by his father's sister who lived outside Paris.

BB's agent Olga Horstig-Primuz then took up the story: '"The aunt has several children of her own," she said. "It is better for him to be there. I cannot tell you exactly where he is because his mother does not want him to have the same attention and publicity that she has had. She feels quite protective about him. Indeed, he is not allowed to give interviews.'''

The *Sunday Express* concluded its report: 'Now Nicolas, who shows an astonishing likeness to his mother right down to the famous pout, is about to leave school. But it is understood that a showbusiness career does not appeal to him. Instead he has set his heart on going to university and is planning to become a lawyer.'

Returning home after the funeral, Brigitte spoke briefly to reporters. What was she doing now, they wanted to know? It was common knowledge that new scripts and offers of films were still being submitted to her agent in Paris, but all were being resolutely turned down. Was she not at all tempted to return to the screen and once more delight her fans, whose numbers and determination to keep her legend alive had never diminished?

'*Non, mais non!*' she declared emphatically, her eyes flashing. 'You see I am very busy now. I wonder how I could live when I was working. I take care of the flowers. I'm very interested in trees. I have learned to cook. I play cards and the guitar. I look after my animals.' Her world was a private one now, she said, before stepping back into the seclusion of *La Madrague*. 'I never read the newspapers – they are so full of *les catastrophes* I prefer not to know. But sometimes I look at TV.'

For a year BB was left to her privacy: drenching herself in the sun, entertaining her friends, spending her days as she pleased. Her years of shrewd investments provided her with enough money not to have to worry where the next franc came from. Shortly before her forty-fifth birthday she agreed to give a short interview to *Radio Française*, and surprised the interviewer by admitting that although her life was generally tranquil she could still make a 'damn nuisance' of herself when aroused. Her hot-temper and impatience had not been cooled by her lack of activity. This apart, though, life with Miroslav was good.

'In four and a half years we've had our ups and downs – but I've never felt like breaking up,' she said, and then added: 'I'd say my life has been pretty positive. After all it's better to be old than dead.'

The question of BB's age – and her looks – was to be a topic that would engage the attention of the press in the following year, and be costly in the case of one particular magazine.

A cheerful Brigitte visiting Strasbourg with Miroslav Brosek to attend a Council of Europe meeting on wildlife conservation in 1978

1980-1981
'My Days are as the Wind Blows Me'

URING THE COURSE of her forty-sixth year, the subject of BB's looks was to engage the pens of a number of journalists. Certain members of the press who had never shared the widespread admiration for her, looked for signs that her beauty was finally departing now that she was in middle-age. The fact that it was not declining to any real degree – as testified by friends who joined her at *La Madrague*, in Paris on the farm at Bazoches or at Meribel – did not deter the detractors.

Brigitte, for her part, made no specific claims, but told one enquirer in the summer of 1980, 'I have everything to make me happy. I am in good health, and I am not too ugly. I am able to live without working. I am delighted with my age,' she added, 'It gives me more presence than I had at twenty-five and more distance to judge life.'

The choice of the word judge was an appropriate one, because in July she had to go to court over what she considered an outrageous attack on her by a Paris magazine. Her face and figure had, of course, been featured on countless thousands of magazine covers over the years, and never had one troubled her. Indeed, most had done much to underline her beauty and photogenic qualities.

But in November 1979, the French monthly magazine *Hara Kiri* had featured on its cover a faked and unflattering photograph of her that made her look as though she had only one tooth. Although some less than complimentary pictures of her had been published in the past – particularly during her long-running battles with the *paparazzi* – this particular example went beyond the realms of acceptability, Brigitte thought, and she instructed her lawyers to sue the magazine.

It was an important case, needless to say. For although public figures are undeniably open to caricature as an element of the publicity they attract – to what limits could this distortion be taken? Both sides defended their points of view, with implications which ran far beyond the outcome of the case itself. Finally, after hours of testimony, claim and counter-claim, the court handed down its judgement. It ruled that the impression of age given by the photograph 'even if it was exaggerated and approaching caricature' was nonetheless of a nature to 'tarnish Brigitte Bardot's image'. The court awarded damages equivalent to £2,105 against *Hara Kiri*. It was another notable achievement for the 'Sex Goddess (Retired)' – as one newspaper put it – and comforted many public figures in France who had been increasingly feeling the press was displaying new lows in bad taste.

The seriousness of the matter was, however, speedily relieved by an amusing little story from London where an autographed photograph of BB – showing her in all her stunning beauty – caused a stir of interest because of the dedication scrawled across it. The picture, which was actually a postcard, was addressed to one Malcolm Agnew and read: 'Mon cherie, J'ai pense dat you would wish a leetle snapp shott of me. I mees you . . .'

The card turned up at Sotheby's in London as part of the collection of the 'king of autograph hunters', Ray Rawlins, which was being auctioned. Listed as Lot 912 it was described as 'Bardot (Brigitte). Autographed postcard signed, postmark 2/3 May 1961 to Malcolm Agnew.'

Who, though, was Malcolm Agnew? And what had been going on between him and BB in 1961? Bardot-watchers who thought they knew about *all* of BB's liaisons, had never heard of this man so passionately addressed in best Franglais. Was the card a joke?

The *Evening Standard* took up the mystery. 'I called Sotheby's,' the Diarist 'Londoner' reported. 'My enquiries elicited some alarm. The postcard had been accepted by the auctioneers in good faith, because it came from such an impressive collection. "But we must admit that examples of Miss Bardot's handwriting are extremely rare," I was told.'

Thus began the *Affaire BB* at Sotheby's. But, sadly, it was never resolved for after waiting some weeks for fresh clues, 'Londoner' reported on 22 August, 'Sotheby's has decided that Lot 912 is not what it was catalogued to be and it has been withdrawn from sale.' The columnist could not resist a footnote, 'Brigitte Bardot still seems able to raise a blush or two – and cer-

tainly no faces seem to be redder than some at Sotheby's at the moment!'

Within a month, however, there was a rather more serious story about a man in BB's life. Just before her birthday, Brigitte admitted there had been a change in her personal life. She and Miroslav had parted: he had suddenly flown to America, without telling her.

BB was as matter-of-fact about it as ever. 'With my experience, which is quite extensive, I say you can never count on a man,' she said. 'I give myself completely in love. When I discover I am getting nothing in return I am shocked and nothing is the same any more.

'I hate breaking off relationships and always let the man take the initiative. I never see my lovers and husbands again – I have nothing to say to them. Friendship is different. You can meet a friend after two years and like him as much as before,' she added.

Brigitte also revealed that she was still campaigning on behalf of animals, though less publicly than before. She had been to see the French Agricultural Minister during a trip to Paris – for a 'man to man' talk as she charmingly put it – and impressed on him the need for further legislation to protect certain endangered species. If anyone thought her stature was in any way decreased these days, she emphasised pointedly, 'The Cabinet Ministers concerned give me appointments straight away – that's proof, isn't it?'

The belief that BB had now well and truly earned the position of becoming a legend in her own lifetime, was further strengthened early in 1981 when seasons of her films began to be put on not only in France, but in Holland, Germany and Britain, too, while a couple of records she

212

had made in the 1960s were released on the AZ label – 'Harley Davidson' and 'Mister Sun'.

Although now generally disinclined to give lengthy interviews, she did allow herself to be coerced by these signs of public appreciation into talking to France's most influential daily newspaper, *Le Monde*. The interview was conducted on 25 February by Hervé Guibert who found her 'in superb shape, bronzed, and in tight-fitting jeans and black pullover'. What follows is the first appearance in English of her most recent, and arguably most definitive, statement on her life since she made her last feature film. She began by describing how and why she decided to stop acting.

'It was right in the middle of filming *Colinot Trousse-Chemise*,' she said, 'that I decided it would be my last film. I thought that the cinema would do nothing more for me and that I should do nothing more for the cinema – as a couple separates as soon as they have nothing more to say to each other. It was time I stopped filming, for fear of sinking into mediocrity. One ought not, just because one has been successful at a particular moment, to hang on to it all one's life. One cannot, just because destiny has drawn one up to an extraordinary dimension, live all one's life in a dimension which can only diminish. The brilliant becomes the humdrum. Can you imagine Marilyn Monroe playing the mother of a family? One must leave behind a beautiful image of oneself, leave things before they leave you. When I turn a page – whether on the cinema or on a love that has ended – I never turn back. I would have been mad to return to the cinema.'

Brigitte next discussed her career as a whole. 'I made some forty films and I had no life; no private life because of the press,

A rare photograph of Brigitte in the privacy of her home, where she rarely allows cameras to intrude

and because I made film after film. My life was intimately linked to the cinema. There were moments when I enjoyed acting, but it was never an obsession. I have never been an actress at heart. Real actresses cannot stop acting. They must act until they die.

'For me the most exciting moment was the end of the day, when everything stopped. Some days, after filming, I would go to the studio to make a record. I sang for my own pleasure, as a recreation, never as an extra job. One must sometimes do things solely because one wants to. Nowadays people work only for the money, there is no longer any joy in creating, only interest and interest is limited. The cinema is a part of my life that is dead. I have no time to live with my memories. Sometimes I see my films again, when they are shown on television and they make me laugh. I have certainly made some bad choices, but I have no regrets.'

BB admitted that her fame from these pictures had enabled her to do many things she really wanted to do. And even now this fame showed no signs of diminishing.

'I have never received so much mail as I do now,' she said, 'not even at the height of my career. At the time of *La Vérité*, for instance, or even other important films, I did not receive so many letters – whole post-bags full – many of them from the young, from seven to twenty-year-olds. They probably do not even know the name of one of my films. They do not know me through the cinema, either. When they hear the name of Brigitte Bardot, it is no longer synonymous with a star or a sex-symbol, but with animal protection. This passion has always been a part of me, I have always loved and defended animals, but I hadn't the time before. I was at first the prisoner of anonymity, then of the films I was making. Working for animals is not labour, it is almost a ministry, there are no time limits, just as there are no limits to suffering.'

Turning to her own life, she went on: 'I can no longer enjoy myself as I did before. I have seen too many horrors to feel free. It is difficult to get away from certain images. Formerly I was amused by a trifle, like a child. I laughed as I walked, I laughed as I danced. There were moments when life was good, but with simple things. One did not go in search of complicated things, drugs or way-out sects; one did not bother to pierce one's cheek with a nappy-pin or let one's hair grow down to the waist like Jesus Christ.

'I meet fewer and fewer funny people, who can tell comical stories, who are naturally jolly. Music, too, is less jolly – New Orleans jazz and the Charleston sparkled like fireworks. Now, the longer it goes on, the less musical it is, and the more noisy. The noise hides everything, it is the echo of a cry of sadness. I feel it is very good to laugh in life, one must laugh. I do not mean that one must tickle oneself all the time to make oneself laugh, but the underlying joy of living that everyone should have in his heart of hearts is replaced by a false sort of collective jolliness which explodes in the noise of nightclubs. There is no time to be bored. When I was twenty, life was certainly easier than it is for the young today. It seems as if the government takes pleasure in making it complicated, and clogs it with all sorts of responsibilities which leave no room for a carefree existence. There is no longer such a thing as a carefree existence.'

Finally, Herve Guibert asked her what the future held for her. 'I have left Paris,' she said. 'I live in St. Tropez, in the sun, in the open air, and by the sea. I find it very difficult to put up with Paris crowds. I do not like traffic jams, the cattle mentality, putting coins in machines, driving round to find somewhere to park, arriving late for an appointment. Life becomes a struggle, a way of existence that no longer means anything. Nasty smells, concrete everywhere, not knowing what season it is because one cannot see the trees, I find all this very depressing.

'The most beautiful thing in life *is* life – it really is life. And one must realise it. Life is for lots of things, and above all for realising that one is alive. If you took a census, you would find that three-quarters of the people do not realise that they are alive. For me, every morning when I wake up is a new one. My days are never the same, if they were I should no longer be alive, I should become a robot. My days are as the wind blows me.'

These certainly sound like the words of a woman who has found much of the contentment she has so long sought. Some aspects of her life may well still hold those dark fears that have always dogged her footsteps, but there is now about her a general air of peace and calm. Perhaps the attainment of this state of mind has given her the impetus to do what she has for so long considered inconceivable. To go back in front of the cameras. This latest development in her remarkable life and legend forms what is reluctantly the last chapter of *this* book, but could well be the start of a whole new phase of her life . . .

1982
A Legend Reflects...

'I THINK THE FRENCH cinema has become a horror. I no longer watch films, but the few extracts I see on television do not make me want to go back. The cinema has become the reflection of what France has become – something mediocre, commonplace. No more dreams, no more mystery, no more grand feelings.'

These are the words of Brigitte Bardot, speaking in 1981, one of the twentieth century's legendary screen stars, and the woman who almost single-handedly put the French cinema on the world film map. They are strong words – words that some would accept, others deny. But what makes them important is that having said them, BB decided a year later, after resisting it for a decade, to return to films. She it was, of course, who had given the French cinema 'dreams, mystery and grand feelings' – was it now her intention to try and bring them back to the screen once more? Certainly, when it was announced that her return was to be for a three-hour-long film of her own life-story, so replete with those three elements, the possibility was there.

The announcement of the film called *Brigitte Bardot – As She Is*, was made at the MIP-TV French Television Festival at Cannes on 2 May by Pierre Desgraupes, the chief of Channel 2. He said that his company had signed a contract with Brigitte Bardot for a TV special in which she would star as herself.

'The film will retrace one of the most outstanding success stories of our time,' Desgraupes said, 'from her childhood to her acclamation as a star of worldwide fame.'

The Channel 2 press handout explained further: 'After nine years in hiding, BB, a living myth, a legend wearing a halo of universal fame, has agreed to appear in front of the cameras to tell her story – to bear witness to a phenomenon which she knows better than anyone else . . . since it concerns her!'

The release added, 'The series will also show the marvellous serenity of a happy woman who has found, beyond the confines of her cinema fame, a powerful sense of militancy in the service of a noble cause – the cause of animals in distress.' This reference to Brigitte's campaigning for animals provided another clue as to why she had agreed to reappear on the screen. This element of her life was to be given some prominence in the film, Allain Bougrain-Dubourg, the producer, explained.

'She is an indefatigable defender of animals,' he said, 'and the film she produced for television on the slaughter of the baby seals was one of the most impressive I've ever seen. I want to show the real Brigitte Bardot, a deeply human woman, fragile and

217

strong at the same time, divided between her chivalrous sense of justice and her instinctive repulsion against a past which was too noisy and often made her unhappy.'

Brigitte later gave her own version of the events. 'I had great qualms,' she said. 'I believed I would die if I had to go through all the business of filming again. But Alain was very persuasive about making the film and he does have his own wildlife programme on Channel 2. So I knew I had to do it for him.'

The French movie magazine, *Ciné Revue*, could also take some credit for this return, for it had recruited her aid in a petition amongst its readers about the need for greater animal protection. The magazine carried this rather breathless report in its issue of 6 May: 'The great return of Brigitte Bardot in front of the cameras came about in a very nice way – which also does us credit – in the offices of *Ciné Revue!* It was not because of her brilliant career that the event took place in our office, but for the sake of the animal cause. In fact, when Brigitte Bardot decided to go to Brussels to meet the Minister of Justice Jean Gol in order to hand over to him the 430,000 signatures of our readers in Belgium, she was followed, for the first time, by the team who will make these films which we shall see at the end of the year on Channel 2.

'It was at *Ciné Revue* that BB found herself for the first time in nine years surrounded by a film crew. The production team of the Sygma Agency, led by Catherine Poubeau, had decided to include in the film this marvellous action by Brigitte Bardot in support of suffering animals. For this campaign led jointly by *Ciné Revue* and Brigitte Bardot, aroused enormous enthusiasm and almost a million signatories for our petition. Mme

Bardot, who was very moved by the thousands of messages of support which reached her, also went to Paris to plead her cause before Mme Edith Cresson, the French Minister of Agriculture.

'The first sequence of this film was therefore the very moving meeting between Brigitte Bardot, nicknamed "The Animals' Fairy Godmother" by our young readers, and officials of the magazine bearing the hundreds of thousands of signatures collected by all those who responded to her appeal in these pages. Our team were privileged to witness the return of BB in front of the cameras for this extraordinary film-autobiography, and were able to see that the woman of today has no need to envy the star of yesterday: the same heart, the same intelligence, the same gentle simplicity which make her far more than a sex symbol or a legend of the cinema.

'The film will be above all else a thrilling human story of a successful life. For the most beautiful gift that BB could give to her admirers is to reveal herself at last as she really is . . .'

Ciné Revue had launched its appeal 'Save Tortured Animals' on 11 March with the aim of obtaining one million signatures, and by the end of April were only 200,000 short of the target. The 800,000 names collected were almost equally divided between French and Belgian readers. These people had responded to a call from the magazine to help put a stop to vivisection and uncontrolled animal experiments. 'Those who govern us,' the magazine had thundered, 'prefer to vote for taxes and bureaucratic regulations rather than laws to protect the lives of defenceless creatures, and show no enthusiasm for the cause of animals – those unfortunates who lack the good fortune to possess the right to vote . . .'

In its issue of 22 April, *Ciné Revue* charted Brigitte's work for animals over the previous six years, including her efforts on behalf of baby seals 'massacred in front of their mothers' and attempts to stop laboratory experiments 'which torture thousands of animals to test commercial products'. 'With a courage which commands respect,' said an editorial, 'she has stood up to the calumnies and dirty tricks which her humanitarian actions have often caused.' The magazine went on: 'Your signatures, arriving by whole postbags full, are so many warnings to those who are withholding the political power to decide on change, and are continuing to practise the policy of the ostrich. With these documents, which show without any possible argument the popular support for Brigitte Bardot's action, "The Animals' Fairy Godmother" will perhaps be able at last to obtain concrete and decisive measures to win the greatest battle of her life.'

Ciné Revue also ran an interview with Brigitte in which she expounded further on her hopes for the future. Here are some of the questions posed by Gérard Neves, and her replies.

GN: For six years you have been fighting ceaselessly in defence of animals. You have been criticised. You have achieved some results, but you have often been disappointed. Are you sometimes disheartened?

BB: Yes, this struggle *is* disheartening! But the sort of letters that I have read restore my morale and warm my heart! They do a lot of good. They give me fresh spirit for the fight. I often need it, for it can be very depressing . . .

GN: What depresses you most?

BB: The fact that even with all the people who signed our appeal and my own interventions, we always seem to be banging our heads against a sort of concrete wall, an inertia which the administration alone has the power to change. So we just have to begin all over again – that is what I do.

GN: You were touched, I believe, by the number of young people who responded to your appeal in *Ciné Revue?*

BB: Yes, the young are marvellous! The fact that this is discussed in schools is very good. The young have fantastic reactions: they are involved, they battle, they collect signatures. The young understand what is at stake: they are fighting for tomorrow. Tomorrow's population will certainly be ten times better than today's, for it will be more *involved*. The young know that there are things that cannot be accepted.

GN: Does it not strike you as odd that we have created ministries of the environment, of the quality of life, of leisure, but never a ministry of animals?

BB: I will tell you this: nobody really bothers about them! There is no ministry of animal defence, of animal protection. People talk more about nature and the quality of life because we are beginning to understand realities. But the simple problem of animal suffering was not recognised until quite late, and then by the Ministry of Agriculture. The Ministry of the Environment, for example, is only concerned with wild fauna as far as animals are concerned. I mean, what matters to them is not so much how animals may suffer, but how they may disappear!

219

And in the end, if the animal suffers while disappearing, the Ministry of Environment doesn't care. *Suffering* is the concern of the Ministry of Agriculture!

Something which is also important, I believe, is the role of the various mediums of communication. In scholastic circles they have not yet begun to teach respect for life in all its forms. Only a little is talked about animals, but there is much on respect for the little classmate, or respect for the neighbour in the street – the respect for others in general. But if this is not yet being done in school, at least magazines like yours are making people aware. And in the long run, they probably have much more power than the administration!

Nowadays, what is the administration doing? It is only following the campaigns of the media. It is only made to stir itself when it has its back to the wall and realises that it can no longer remain inactive! All the major problems which are not immediately economic can only be resolved by the pressure of public opinion. Only then will the administration react. It never takes the lead, for it considers that there are other priorities, and in the end it finds itself overtaken by priorities which it never dreamed of the day before. Let us hope that the animals will be the next priority!

GN: When readers call you 'The Animals' Fairy Godmother' are you pleased?

BB: Yes, because I am very sensitive. They turn to me because I take things to heart, more than a society like the SPA, which is snowed under and which does not know which way to turn. Sometimes I am really sad. I lack courage. Then, reactions like those encountered by your campaign cheer me up, because the love which your readers have for animals is terrific.

People think that I have power to resolve problems, but I have no power. They say to me: 'I have written to the minister, to the SPA, to the powers that be. But it is no good, so I have come to you!' I would do what they ask if I could, but I have no power . . .

GN: But, still, doors are open to you . . .

BB: Yes, they are open, but not as much as people imagine! However, there have been positive things: I had a laboratory closed. There was the organisation of the transport of horses coming from Poland. But there is still great suffering unworthy of man.

GN: Do you see these as a stage towards victory for the defenders of animals?

BB: Yes, but only symbolic! The results are less tangible, but still a sort of victory. There are experimenters in laboratories whose attitudes are changing. You can't measure them, but they do exist. They are growing ashamed of their work, because it is talked about in their families or among their friends. I know some children whose mother

Brigitte and friend – a photograph that epitomises her love of animals

220

worked in a laboratory doing animal experiments. They asked her about them and she was ashamed to answer. After she had heard them, she promised not to experiment on rabbits any more. Only rats! That seems a little stupid, I know, for the result is minimal – but it proves that attitudes *can* be changed.

These are the kind of things I think about when I am discouraged. They are little things, but still count a lot for the animals. Making people realise about their suffering is a big step forward to a more vigorous campaign against animal misery.

But I still demand to know why the authorities continue to turn away from the cries of those millions of animals who are suffering such agony.

Aside from the undoubted effect this interview had on readers – as well as underlining the strength of Brigitte's feelings – it firmly dispelled the stories that certain French newspapers had promoted that the great BB was now a virtual recluse – hiding behind the high walls of *La Madrague*, her beauty fading fast, and refusing to see anyone. A lonely creature with only her dogs and animals to keep her company.

Then, when Roger Vadim, who had been living in America for a number of years, returned to France to begin a new project in the summer of 1982, this rumour was firmly laid to rest. As one of BB's oldest friends, it was only natural that Vadim should visit her. It proved a delightful reunion for this couple whose lives and careers have been so inextricably entwined: who together took the film world by storm and wrote a new chapter in cinema history. Their meeting also brings our story neatly full circle.

The legend of BB had, of course, begun when the Russian exile Plemiannikov met the elfin-faced teenager from the bourgeois Parisian family. So could this new phase of her life as she completed thirty years as a film star, and neared her fiftieth birthday – have any better entré than their meeting once again? That she was also back behind the cameras which Vadim had seen as her destiny all those years ago made it doubly apposite.

When the couple swopped reminiscences, they discovered both were involved in exciting new projects. Vadim, after a period of inactivity, was returning to France to make a film entitled *The Day of the Young Girls*, about the lives of a group of French youngsters in a small town in the fifties. It was clearly an idea that fascinated him, and one he knew would transport him back to those magical years when he launched BB on an unsuspecting world and changed the lives of just such young girls as he was going to portray. A return to his film roots, in fact. And from Brigitte he learned that by a strange twist of fate she, too, had chosen this moment to go back to her roots.

Vadim reported: 'She is writing her memoirs. I gather she intends taking several years to do it. But she has the time . . . I told her she would have to be careful about the things she said about people in her book. She just laughed. "I'm going to tell the truth about everyone," she said, "starting with myself. If I do that I think it gives me the right to say what I want about others."'

Though fully aware that he would feature prominently in the book, Vadim had no qualms about what BB might say. 'Oh, no. I am not at risk there,' he said. 'When we were married we fought like lovers but there was no animosity. We always liked

222

each other and we still do. In fact when the book is nearly finished, I have promised to help her polish it.'

After his visit, Brigitte recriprocated her former husband's feelings. 'I've still got a strong affection for Vadim. He liberated me from my family. He was my first love. But I was young then. I'm not young any more, but I've never had a facelift as some people may say!'

And her memoirs? Yes, she said, she was writing them, 'mainly when it's raining', but not for the money. 'Money doesn't worry me any more. And nor does life for that matter. You see death is like love. A romantic episode. I thought my life was over when the Church denounced me. They put out pictures of me depicting me as all that is evil. But I'm not evil. Sunbathing in the nude is now an accepted thing, even in England. Perhaps I was before my time?'

Before her time? Brigitte Bardot was certainly an integral part *of* her time, and one of the dominant figures in the history of the late fifties and sixties – her fame justifiably enduring to this day. And as to the future, there seems no doubt that her star status is assured and her legend established beyond all doubt.

Viva, BB! *Bonne chance*, Brigitte!

Acknowledgements

The number of people and organisations that helped in the creation of this book is almost endless, but I should like to record my thanks to the following for information, quotations and photographs: the members of staff of the British Film Institute, London; the British Newspaper Library, Colindale; and the Bibliothèque Nationale de Paris. Also Roger Vadim, Willie Frischauer, Dirk Bogarde, Joan Harrison, Logan Gourlay, Donald Zec, Renaud de Laborderie, Sacha Distel, Gerald Fairlie, Simone de Beauvoir, Louis Malle, Marguerite Duras, Peter Evans, Bernard Valéry, Gunther Sachs, Victor Davis, Tony Crawley, Françoise Sagan and George Feifer. Among the many newspapers and magazines I consulted, the following were particularly helpful: *The Daily Express, Daily Mail, UK Press Gazette, Daily Mirror, The Times, The Observer, L'Exprès, Le Monde, Daily Telegraph, Life, Sunday Times, Evening Standard, The Guardian, The Sunday Express, Cahiers du Cinéma, Picturegoer, Cinémonde, Playboy, Ciné-Revue* and *Variety*. Thanks to these film companies for the use of stills from their films: Sport Films, Warner-Pathé, Gaumont-International, Rank Film Distributors, Miracle Films, Gala Films, Renown Pictures, Columbia Pictures, United Artists, Twentieth Century-Fox, MGM Films, Avco Embassy Pictures, American International, Paramount Pictures, Scotia-Barber Distributors, Hemdale Films and Parc Film-Mag Bodard (Paris). Photographs were also supplied by the Keystone Picture Agency, Rex Features, Aquarius, Popperfoto and John Hillelson.